Scotland
Highlands
and Islands

PASSPORT BOOKS
a division of *NTC Publishing Group*
Lincolnwood, Illinois USA

Published by Passport Books, a division of NTC Publishing Group, 4255 West Touhy Avenue, Lincolnwood (Chicago), Illinois 60646-1975 U.S.A.

NTC First edition © 1997

Authors: John Baxter, David Winpenny, Pat and Charles Aithie

Edited by: Guidelines

Original photography: Jim Henderson

Designer: Stuart Perry

First edition published 1996 by Ordnance Survey and AA Publishing.

© Ordnance Survey and The Automobile Association 1996.

Maps © Crown Copyright and Maps © The Automobile Association 1996.

Gazetteer map references are taken from the National Grid and can be used in conjunction with AA and Ordnance Survey maps and atlases. Places featured in this guide will not necessarily be found on the maps at the back of the book.

ISBN 0-8442-4888-0
Library of Congress Catalog Card Number 95-72836

Color origination by Daylight Colour Art Ltd, Singapore.

Printed and bound in Italy by Tipolitografia G. Canale & C. S.p.A. – Turin

The contents of this book are believed correct at the time of printing. Nevertheless, the Publishers cannot accept responsibility for errors or omissions, or for changes in details given.

Contents

Dunnet
Head
Stroma
Duncansby Head
John o' Groats
Melvich
Thurso
Halkirk
Wick
inbrace
Lybster
THERLAND
Helmsdale
Brora
spie
noch
Moray Firth
Spey Bay
Elgin
Banff
Fraserburgh
rn
Peterhead
Grantown-
on-Spey
Inverurie
viemore
*Cairngorm
Mountains*
ABERDEEN
Banchory
Braemar
Stonehaven
o u n t a i n s
Pitlochry
Brechin
Montrose
erfeldy
Forfar
DUNDEE
Arbroath
PERTH
rieff
St Andrews
Cupar
Kirkcaldy
Dunfermline
alkirk
Firth of Forth
EDINBURGH
Dunbar
Livingston
Dalkeith
otherwell
anark
Peebles
Galashiels
Berwick-upon-Tweed
iggar
Selkirk
Coldstream
Kelso
Hawick
Jedburgh
Alnwick
Moffat

Shetland Islands
Herma
Ness
Unst
Yell Sound
Yell
Fetlar
Esha Ness
*St Magnus
Bay*
Mainland
Whalsay
Foula
Lerwick
West
Burra
Bressay
Sumburgh Head

0		20		40 km
0	10	20	30 miles	

Fair Isle

**THE
NORTHERN ISLES**

Orkney Islands
North
Ronaldsay
Papa Westray
Westray
Sanday
Rousay
Eday
Stronsay
Mainland
Shapinsay
Stromness
Kirkwall
*Scapa
Flow*
Hoy
South Ronaldsay
Pentland Firth

0	20 km
0	10 miles

Introducing The Scottish Highlands and Islands

INTRODUCING THE SCOTTISH HIGHLANDS AND ISLANDS

One of the last truly unspoilt areas of Europe, the Highlands and Islands cover about half of Scotland. The Highlands are probably most famous for their dramatic and colourful landscape – the Cairngorms, Glencoe, and the Nevis Range; more unexpected, perhaps, are the gardens of the west coast, where palm trees and exotic flowering shrubs flourish, warmed by the Gulf Stream. Sheltered sandy beaches are surprisingly frequent, not least on the extraordinarily beautiful islands of Harris and Barra.

Britain's largest mammal, the red deer, forages in the Highlands, beneath the eye of the eagle; there are hides from which to view ospreys, and dolphins abound in the Moray Firth. Vast lochs and majestic rivers are home to the best salmon and trout.

OSPREY
Above, ospreys, hunted almost to extinction, returned to Scotland in 1955 and may be seen in summer at the RSPB's Loch Garten reserve

HAGGIS
Haggis (left) with potato and 'bashed neeps' is the traditional dish; haggis and chips is widely available

CALLANISH STANDING STONES
The Highlands have a legacy of mysterious standing stones and prehistoric monuments, none finer than the stone circle of Callanish on Lewis, above

WOOLLEN MILL
As souvenirs of Scotland go, you can't do much better than a thick tartan rug – picnic on it on a sunny brae, or wrap up warm on a chilly Highland night

NESSIE
Left, The Loch Ness Monster has been avoiding unwanted attention for years

PANNING FOR GOLD
Helmsdale once had its very own gold rush, and you may still find flecks of gold in Highland streams

REINDEER
Right, reindeer at the Cairngorm Reindeer Centre near Aviemore lead a busy life, talking to summer tourists and doubling for Rudolph at Christmas

WHISKY
Left, for a drop of really fine whisky, the Highland malts take a lot of beating – judge for yourself on the Strathspey Whisky Trail

TEN BEST BOAT TRIPS
Moray Firth
Kylerhea ferry
Loch Coruisk
Loch Ness
Uig ferry
Unst ferry
Small Isles
Corran ferry
Kyles of Bute
Loch Lomond

THE ESSENCE OF THE SCOTTISH HIGHLANDS AND ISLANDS
If you have little time and want to sample the essence of the Highlands and Islands:
Enjoy the romantic beauty of Eilean Donan Castle on Loch Duich, and charming Plockton... **Watch** the sun setting low over the Mull of Kintyre... **Take** the little Mull and West Highland Narrow Gauge Railway to the delightful Torosay Castle... **Enjoy** the peace of the Iona Community... **Hop** on a ferry to the Small Isles or the Summer Isles, or go whale and dolphin watching... **Indulge** yourself at the Loch Fyne Oyster Bar... **Drive** up the pass of Bealaach-na-Ba, or take the Aviemore ski-lift for spectacular views... **Take** in the history of whaling and fishing at Orkney's Stromness Museum... **Feel** on the edge of the world at Duncansby Head or Cape Wrath... **Follow** the trail of Bonnie Prince Charlie to Glenfinnan and Culloden, then back again to Skye and the Outer Hebrides... **Admire** the gardens at Inverewe and the wilderness of Assynt.

AN ORKNEY CHAIR
Left, canny Orkney weavers developed a draught-proof chair – one of the exhibits at Kirbister farm museum

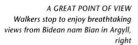

BONNIE PRINCE CHARLIE
Highland history is shot through with the Jacobite uprising of 1745 and its grim aftermath, tied in with the thwarted ambitions of the romantic and charismatic Prince Charles Edward Stuart

SHEEP ON THE ROAD
On the narrow roads of northern Scotland, sheep treat the road with a certain carelessness, so beware!

A GREAT POINT OF VIEW
Walkers stop to enjoy breathtaking views from Bidean nam Bian in Argyll, right

A Weekend in The Scottish Highlands and Islands: Day One

For many of us a weekend is the most that can be managed as a break in busy lives. These four pages offer an itinerary designed to ensure that you see and enjoy the very best of the Scottish Highlands, including a trip to Skye. Places within the gazetteer are in **bold**.

Friday Night

Make your way to the **Isle of Skye** and stay, if you can, at Kinloch Lodge, Lord and Lady Macdonald's secluded Edwardian lodge at Isle Ornsay. It is mainly the food which draws people here. Cookery writer Lady Macdonald uses only the best Scottish produce for her sumptuous dinners, taken in the elegant dining room under the watchful gaze of the family portraits.

There is plenty of alternative accommodation on Skye, but much of it, including Kinloch Lodge, closes down in the depths of winter, so check in advance.

Saturday Morning

Drive north on the A851 to Broadford, then turn left on to the B8083 and follow this minor road down to Elgol for wonderful scenery all along the way. Return the same way to Broadford, turn left and take the A850 north, turning left on to the A863 beyond Sconser. Follow this winding route up the west coast, turning left at Kilmuir on to the B884 for Colbost.

Enjoy breath-taking views of the Cuillins, above

Left: At Sligachan take the road west across the neck of Skye

Below, pause for refreshment at the popular Sligachan Hotel

Fortify yourself with traditional Scottish fare, right

Explore the attractions of Dunvegan Castle, below

Saturday Lunch

The Three Chimneys restaurant at Colbost is in a remote and beautiful corner of Skye, overlooking Loch Dunvegan. Within this converted crofter's cottage you can enjoy well-cooked food based on good local ingredients. The lunchtime menu includes some traditional Scottish dishes.

Saturday Afternoon

If there is time, have a look at the Black House Folk Museum at Colbost before driving back to Kilmuir and turning left for Dunvegan. Dunvegan Castle has been the seat of the McCleod clan chiefs for nearly 800 years. The family history can be traced from its Norse origins to the present day through relics, books, pictures, arms – and don't miss the legendary Fairy Flag.

Try to fit in one of the boat trips to see brown seals at close range, basking on the skerries in front of the castle.

Saturday Night

From Dunvegan drive across the island to Kyleakin and cross the road bridge to Kyle of Lochalsh on the mainland.

Drive north east for about five miles (8 km) to the picture-postcard village of Plockton and stay at the enchanting Haven Hotel, where you will be pampered with fine food and accommodation of a very high standard.

Seek out the delights of award-winning Plockton, right

A Weekend in the Scottish Highlands and Islands: Day Two

Our second day is spent back on the mainland, venturing northwards through Glenshieldaig Forest, along Loch Torridon and Loch Maree and on to visit one of the most famous gardens in the country.

Sunday Morning

From Plockton, drive east through Achmore to join the A890, turning left to drive through Stromeferry and along the southern shore of Loch Carron.

Around the head of the loch, turn left on to the A896 and follow this road back along the north shore, before turning inland and heading north across the Applecross peninsula, through Glenshieldaig Forest and on to **Torridon**.

Here, amidst some of Scotland's finest mountain scenery, is the excellent Countryside Centre. It isn't open until the afternoon, but you can stop to look at the deer museum and to view the herd of red deer kept on the estate.

Drive on up Glen Torridon, turning left on to the A832 and continuing along the shores of Loch Maree before reaching **Gairloch**.

Pass through the exquisite scenery of Loch Carron, left

Visit the Countryside Centre at Torridon, below

Bottom, follow in Queen Victoria's footsteps by Loch Maree

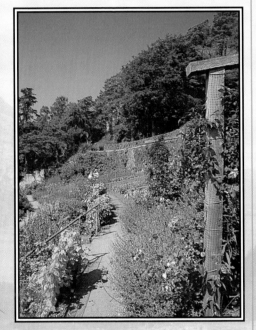

Sunday Lunch

Stop at The Old Inn in Gairloch for lunch. It is a former coaching inn overlooking the fishing harbour and has real ales and a good range of food.

Don't worry if your morning has been more leisurely than intended – food is available all day at the Old Inn's bistro.

Sunday Afternoon

It is only a short distance from Gairloch to Poolewe, where **Inverewe Garden** is renowned for its sub-tropical plants, which flourish in the Atlantic Drift climate. The garden is at its best in early June, but there is great beauty here at any time between March and October.

Sunday Night

A weekend in such a remote part of north-west Scotland will need a third overnight stay before you head for home.

Retrace your route back down Loch Maree to Kinlochewe, then carry straight on to Achnasheen. Here you will find Ledgowan Lodge, a delightfully friendly country house hotel in wooded grounds.

From here it is an easy drive eastwards to **Inverness**, or you can take a more convoluted route south west towards **Fort William**. A direct route due south is, unfortunately, not an option.

Take in lunch at Gairloch, top, before going on to visit the extraordinary garden of Inverewe, above

Right, enjoy a last view of Ben Slioch, on Loch Maree, before heading homewards

Argyll and Kintyre

Easily accessible from Glasgow, the peninsulas and islands of Argyll spill west and south from the Clyde, with the sea a constant presence. Here the many faces of Scotland come together – rugged mountains and sparkling lochs, fertile farmland and forest, busy fishing villages and remote cottages. The past is ever present too, with prehistoric remains all around and the cradle of Celtic Christianity on the island of Iona. All of these attractions are linked by roads through high passes and by ferries that shuttle across sometimes choppy straits.

DOWN IN THE FOREST

Argyll Forest Park has stretches of open moorland and bare mountain tops as well as trees. Where conifer planting has taken place, you can still find pockets of ancient woodland, like that near Glenbranter, or more exotic species like the Tasmanian eucalyptus trees at Kilmun, the result of Forestry Commission experiments. The 53,630 acres of the Park produce 70,000 tonnes of timber each year, mostly for paper and saw mills in Scotland. The forest is home to varied wildlife – only the luckiest visitor will see a golden eagle or a wildcat, but buzzards and sparrowhawks are easier to spot, and you may get a glimpse of deer, foxes or even the rare red squirrel.

The long blue finger of Loch Eck lies at the heart of the Argyll Forest Park

ARGYLL FOREST PARK Strathclyde

The towering, pine-clad mountains, deep valleys and narrow lochs of the Argyll Forest Park, established more than 60 years ago, are a perfect introduction to the area. You can reach the heart of the Park up Glen Croe, with the 'Arrocher Alps' to the north, of which Ben Arthur, 'The Cobbler', is the most distinctive peak. From Rest-and-be-Thankful an exciting single-track road descends Hell's Glen to Lochgoilhead, from where there are waymarked walks, including one to Rob Roy's Cave. Further down Loch Goil are the impressive remains of Carrick Castle, a 14th-century tower house.

Mountain-bikers should head for Ardgartan and Glenbranter, where they will find signed mountain-bike trails. The latter is also the start point of the delightful Lauder Forest Walks (music-hall entertainer Sir Harry Lauder once owned the land), which go through old oak woodland and rare rhododendrons to a series of

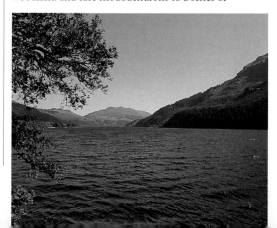

waterfalls. The best-known of the trails is up Puck's Glen, at the foot of Lock Eck, crossing many bridges through a steep, tree-lined gorge. It originally led to a folly built by the Youngers of Benmore, whose estate is now the Younger Botanic Garden. This outpost of Edinburgh's Royal Botanic Garden has high rainfall and a mild climate – ideal conditions for growing rhododendrons. There are more than 650 different types here, which make a visit in early summer a spectacular treat, but there is interest throughout the season, with conifers of all types, and paths that zig-zag up the mountainside to spectacular viewpoints. Most famous of all is the avenue of Redwoods, planted in 1863 – the trees are now more than 100 feet (30.5 metres) tall.

BUTE Strathclyde

Bute has been the holiday playground for generations of Glaswegians, most of whom have arrived at Rothesay on the ferry from Wemyss Bay. Finely set on the Firth of Clyde, Rothesay has a turn-of-the-century atmosphere created by its solid, mostly Victorian houses and decorative Winter Gardens, but much more ancient are the impressive ruins of the moated 13th-century Rothesay Castle.

The island largely consists of green and fertile hills, with superb views across the narrow Kyles of Bute to the mainland and to mountainous Arran – Ettrick Bay has an especially beautiful aspect. Further down the west coast are the ruins of a 6th-century chapel, overlooking Inchmarnock Island, while in the more mountainous area south of Bute is the mainly 12th-century St Blane's Chapel, set in a bowl of rocks on the site of a Celtic monastery. Just off the road up the east coast is one of Bute's hidden gems, the extraordinary Victorian Gothic Mount Stewart House, surrounded by gardens that lead down to the shore.

THE ULTIMATE CONVENIENCE

Since 1899 the needs of gentlemen visiting Rothesay Pier have been met in a modest building which hides a spectacular interior. Go through the etched glass door and you are in a temple of cloacal magnificence. Fourteen stalls, of white enamel, surrounded with sea-green imitation marble, stand along the wall, while six more form a central feature. The nine cubicles retain their panelled doors and wooden seats, and there is well-polished copper piping and gleaming embossed tile-work everywhere. Fittings were supplied at the cost of £530 by Twyfords of Glasgow; recent restoration cost nearly £30,000, and makes the modest entrance fee a bargain. Only the boldest ladies can see this splendour; the Victorians made no provision for them, and their adjoining facility is modern.

The royal burgh of Rothesay, Bute

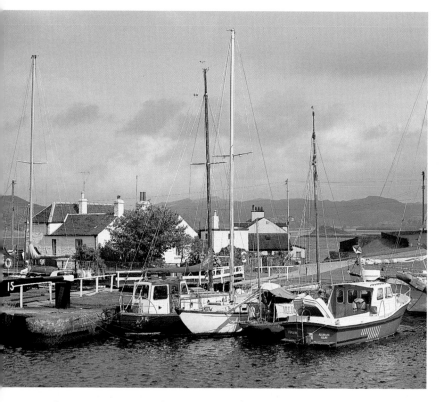

Small craft shelter in the canal basin at Crinan

PARA AND THE PUFFERS

Para Handy, captain of the 'puffer' *Vital Spark*, first made his appearance in the *Glasgow Evening News* in 1905. Neil Munroe's stories, set during the early 1900s, have been enjoyed by readers – and television viewers – ever since. The Crinan Canal and Loch Fyne are the heart of Para Handy country, with comic forays to Campbeltown, Mull, Arran, and frequently to Glasgow. *Vital Spark* was one of the largest of three kinds of puffers – steam-driven vessels, that get their name from the puffing noise made by the engine exhaust venting through the funnel.

CRINAN CANAL Strathclyde

In 1847 Queen Victoria and Prince Albert sailed the nine miles (14.5 km) of the Crinan Canal aboard the barge *Sunbeam* – a journey used later in the century by MacBrayne's steamers to sell 'Royal Route' excursions from Glasgow to Oban. Today you are most likely to see pleasure craft negotiating the canal's 15 locks, but its purpose was to enable merchant traffic to and from the Western Isles to avoid the voyage around the Mull of Kintyre. Two famous engineers worked on the Crinan Canal, which opened in 1801. Rennie did the original engineering work, and Telford solved problems with the water supply.

From the basin at Ardrishaig, where it leaves Loch Fyne, the canal hugs the wooded hillsides as it winds up to its highest point of 64 feet (19.4 metres). On the hills above Cairnbaan are reservoirs that constantly replenish the water in the canal as it descends under the unusual hand-wound rolling bridge at Dunadry. Beyond here the landscape opens out into the flat marshland of the River Add estuary and then into Loch Crinan. The canal ends at the picturesque Crinan Harbour, with beautiful views over the Sound of Jura. With luck you may find a 'puffer' in the harbour to remind you of the canal's past glories.

DUNOON Strathclyde Map ref NS1776

Paddle steamers used to bring huge crowds from Gourock to Dunoon, and there are still regular ferry services here. On the grassy headland between the town's two bays are the remains of the 13th-century royal castle, largely destroyed in 1685. Below is the 1896 statue of Burns's love, Highland Mary, marking the centenary of the poet's death. Dunoon is busiest in late August for the Cowal Highland Gathering, when more than 150 pipe bands from all over the world compete for prestigious trophies.

Morag's Fairy Glen, off the road south from Dunoon, has shaded walks along the Berry Burn, but for more expansive views, continue to Toward Point lighthouse (not open) at the southern end of the A815, where you can look out across the water to Bute and down to Largs. In the grounds of the 19th-century Castle Toward, now an education centre, is a ruined 15th-century tower house, somewhat confusingly called Toward Castle. One of the worst atrocities of the Civil War began here, when Campbell of Ardkinglas besieged the Lamonts, who were Stuart loyalists. Although guaranteed safety, 36 Lamont men were taken to Dunoon and hanged – a monument in Tom-a-Mhoid Road marks the place.

Just north of Dunoon at Lochan Wood is the attractive Cowal Bird Garden, and this area is rich in ancient sites. Near Sandbank, on the shore of Holy Loch, are the huge stones forming Adam's Grave, a Neolithic burial chamber, and you can follow a trail from near Ardnadam Farm to see ancient field boundaries and the site of a prehistoric enclosure.

ON THE OCEAN WAVERLEY

The world's last sea-going paddle streamer, *Waverley*, is a regular visitor to Dunoon and other ports along the Clyde coast. Launched on the Clyde in 1947 and in service until 1973, she was bought for just £1 by the Paddle Steamer Preservation Society. Following restoration, she now regularly plies to and fro across the Clyde during the summer, carrying up to 950 passengers. *Waverley*, with its two distinctive black, red and white funnels, is 240 feet (73.2 metres) long and 57 feet (17.4 metres) broad across the paddle wheels, which are 14 feet (4.2 metres) in diameter. Powered by a 2,100-horsepower steam engine, the vessel is a welcome and impressive sight wherever she goes – and that has included four trips around the whole of Great Britain.

Genteel pleasure gardens adorn the front at Dunoon

CAILEIN MOR

The Dukes of Argyll are descended from the 12th-century Colin Campbell of Loch Awe, known as Cailein Mor – Great Colin. All his successors as clan chief have been designated MacCailein Mor – Great Colin's Son, and they become successively Earls, Marquesses and Dukes of Argyll. The 1st Marquess hedged his bets in the Civil War, crowning Charles II at his Scottish coronation in 1651, but subsequently supporting Cromwell. He and his son were executed for treason at the Restoration, but by the end of the century the 11th Earl was supporting William and Mary, and the dukedom was his reward. The Dukes are Hereditary Great Masters of the Household in Scotland and their baton of office, topped with a royal Scottish lion, is on display in the castle.

Splendid slatey-blue pepperpot towers adorn Inveraray Castle

INVERARAY Strathclyde Map ref NN0908

Inveraray, on the shores of Loch Fyne, is as fine an example of town planning as you will find, created by the 3rd Duke of Argyll in the 1740s to sit at the gates of his grand new home. It seems an incredible amount of trouble to go to, just to move your ancestral home by half a mile (0.8 km), but this was, after all, the extravagant 18th century. The little town that he created is stylish, with a wide main street of white-painted houses running up to the classical kirk. On the waterfront are brilliant white arches, one of which leads to All Saints Episcopal Church – climb the bell-tower for a wonderful panoramic view of the town, the castle, the loch and the hills.

Inveraray Castle, now home to the 12th Duke and his family, is a classical building with pointed sash windows and battlements. Inside, its most spectacular feature is the Armoury Hall, the tallest room in Scotland, which is dramatically adorned with pikes, axes, swords and muskets. A tour of the castle includes splendid state rooms with ornate gilded plasterwork, fine furniture and Campbell family portraits.

Moored on the loch side is the three-masted vessel *Arctic Penguin*, upon which you can take a turn at steering, ring the ship's telegraph, visit the engine room and watch archive film of old sailing and steam ships. Inveraray Jail, near the kirk, has thrown open its doors to more willing visitors. In the semi-circular courtroom you can be part of the crowd hearing a trial, and in the 19th-century cells you can try out canvas hammocks and turn the crank machine. You can even see mug-shots of some of the last petty criminals to use the exercise gallery.

ISLAY, JURA, COLONSAY, SCARBA AND GIGHA

Each of these islands on the eastern side of the Minch has its own distinctive character. Jura, for instance, is one of the last remaining areas of true wilderness and is dominated by the three rounded, conical peaks – The Paps of Jura; the highest, Beinn an Oir, rises to 2,572 feet (784 metres). Neolithic standing stones and cairns here date back to 7000BC. Colonsay and Oronsay have their ancient monuments too, and on their west coasts are great expanses of wonderful clean sand, none better than at Kiloran Bay.

Islay is also a very special place, with remote and spectacular coastal scenery, superb hill walking and a distinctive peaty flavour to the 'water of life' distilled here. The island was once the home of the Lords of the Isles, who ruled most of the Western Isles during the 14th and 15th centuries. Their seat was the now ruined Dunivaig Castle, at Lagavulin, with outposts on two small islands in Loch Finlaggan.

Gigha, east of Islay, is the home of the Ogham Stone, with its indecipherable inscription, which was brought from Ireland in pre-Christian times, and there are plenty of standing stones – those at Kilchattan have been endowed with the wonderful name of Fingal's Limpet Hammers. The beautiful gardens at Achamore House (National Trust for Scotland) are especially noted for their dazzling displays of azaleas and rhododendrons.

Scarba, remote and uninhabited, is a small island off the northern tip of Jura, its highest point 1,470 feet (448 metres). It is separated from its larger neighbour by one of the most treacherous pieces of water anywhere in the world – the whirlpool of Corrievreckan. The flood tide rushes through the narrow sound at speeds of up to 8.5 knots before reaching the place where a great pyramidal rock rises from the seabed 719 feet (219 metres) below to a depth of only 95 feet (29 metres), forming the great whirlpool. There are few more awesome examples of raw natural power – the sound can be heard over 10 miles (16.1 km) away.

A secluded bay on the floral island of Gigha

ISLAY WILDLIFE

The shores of Islay provide a wide variety of habitats, with great expanses of sand as in Loch Indaal, rugged wave-exposed rocky coasts in the west and shingle on the southern coast, with small outlying islands where both grey and common seals are to be seen basking in the sun. The island is particularly rich in flora, on the machair and moorland, in the peat bogs and woodlands. About 110 species of birds breed on Islay, including the rare native chough, a member of the crow family, with the same glossy black plumage but its legs and curved beak are a startling red. Islay is most famous as an over-wintering place for geese, with 25,000 barnacle geese and 4,000 Greenland white-fronted geese arriving each October and staying until the following April before returning north to their breeding grounds.

Kilmartin village, at the head of the valley, overlooks a remarkable prehistoric site

DALRIADA AND THE CORONATION STONE

From around 500AD the Scottish kingdom of Dalriada had its capital in the hill fort at Dunadd. There are traces of buildings on the hillside and defensive terraces around the summit. Carved in the rock just outside is an inscription in Ogham script – evidence of Pictish use of the hilltop – as well as a basin and a footprint that may have been used at coronations. Some believe that Aidan was crowned first Christian king in Britain here in 574AD by St Columba, and that the stone used became the Stone of Scone, now part of the coronation chair in Westminster Abbey.

KILMARTIN   Strathclyde Map ref NR8398

The waters of Loch Awe once flowed southwards through the glacier-formed Kilmartin Glen, depositing sediment on the valley floor. The area was occupied from early prehistoric times, when hunters settled here to farm, and the concentration of monuments that they left behind makes this one of the richest archaeological areas in Scotland. At Achnabreck is the largest group of cup-and-ring marked rocks in Britain, but even more impressive remains are to be found further north

The tall, flat-faced Ballymeanoch standing stones and a line of burial cairns stretch towards Kilmartin village. Ri Cruin is a crescent of boulders in a grove, and carvings of axeheads and, possibly, a boat's keel can be seen on the stones. The three Nether Largie cairns are higher – especially the most southerly, with its large chamber topped by huge stone slabs. Central to the site is Temple Wood Circle, begun around 3000BC and modified several times up to 1200BC. Its ring of standing stones was once nearly covered with a cairn of small rocks; an even older cairn by it, recently excavated, had a wooden circle. At Kilmartin church is a collection of fine grave slabs from the 9th to the 16th centuries, some with life-size figures. Carnasserie Castle, further up the valley, is a well-preserved fortified house from the 16th century, built for John Carwell, Bishop of the Isles.

KINTYRE Strathclyde

At the north end of Kintyre and 38 miles (61.2 km) from Campbeltown, Tarbert has colour-washed houses and the remains of a 15th-century tower house on the site of a former royal castle. The Campbeltown road follows the wind-swept west fringe of Kintyre, with wide views over to Jura and Islay, then the hills give way to gentler country towards the handsome port of Campbeltown. By the waterfront is the late 15th-century Campbeltown Cross, and near by an unexpected delight – the 1913 art deco front of the 256-seat Picture House. Davaar Island, reached on foot at low tide, shelters the harbour, and in a cave on its south side is a painting of the crucifixion by Archibald MacKinnon, dating from 1887.

St Columba landed near Southend at the foot of the peninsula – a ruined chapel and two footprints carved in a nearby rock mark the spot. A winding road eastwards goes to the Mull of Kintyre, with its lighthouse – a stark, windswept place, only 12 miles (19.3 km) from Ireland. A single-track, hairpin road with breathtaking views over Arran follows the western coast back to Campbeltown; alternatively retrace your route up the B842, diverting west to Machrihanish, where the golf course is on the bay's edge.

North of Campbeltown, the east coast route is slow and winding, with tree-lined glens and fertile valleys. Up the valley from the battlemented castle by the shore at Saddell are the remains of Saddell Abbey, with its impressive collection of carved gravestones. Carradale, further up the coast, is a small village beside a beautiful sandy bay, while at Skipness you can visit the castle and eat fresh seafood.

DRY LAND SAILORS

Were it not for the mile (1.6 km) of land at Tarbert, Kintyre would be an island. Before the Crinan Canal was built, fishermen would sometimes carry ships on rollers across the isthmus to avoid the long sea journey around the Mull of Kintyre. King Robert Bruce, too, had his ships dragged across to make a surprise attack on Castle Sween. But the most famous traverse at Tarbert was made in 1198 by the Norwegian king, Magnus Barelegs. Promised by King Malcolm Canmore of Scotland that he could include in his kingdom any island he could navigate around, Magnus had his men haul his boat over the land, while he sat at the tiller beneath the billowing sails, thus adding Kintyre to his possessions.

The high lantern tower of Tarbert's church would have acted as a navigational beacon for sailors around Kintyre

Near the ruined Kilchurn Castle, the waters of Loch Awe are shallow and reedy

MOUNTAIN POWER

Ben Cruachan holds a secret – Scotland's first big pump storage power station. The Visitor Centre explains how water from an artificial loch high up on the mountain is fed down through the rock to turbines within the mountain. Off-peak power is used to pump the water back up to the reservoir. The highlight of a visit is a ¾-mile (1.2-km) ride down tunnels to the huge turbine hall, 300 feet (91.4 metres) long and 120 feet (36.6 metres) high. The plants along the way are real – tropical species, which are thriving happily in the artificial light, heat and humidity of the tunnels.

LOCH AWE   Strathclyde Map ref NN1227

Glacial action reversed the waters of Loch Awe to flow through the dramatic Pass of Brander instead of through Kilmartin Glen. The longest loch in Scotland – nearly 25 miles (40.2 km), more than a mile (1.6 km) longer than Loch Ness – it is very narrow, and the north end is dominated by the peak of Ben Cruachan. You can take a steamboat trip from Lochawe village which includes the impressive ruins of Kilchurn Castle, set on what was once an island. Ardanaiseig Gardens, 4 miles (6.4 km) west of Kilchrenan, are full of glowing rhododendrons and specimen trees beside the eastern shore of the loch. It is worth following the minor road south through Inverliever Forest, which offers forest walks and spectacular high viewpoints over the loch. The western shore road gives views of the loch's small islands, some with ancient chapels and burial grounds.

LOCHGILPHEAD   Strathclyde Map ref NR8688

Lochgilphead was once the centre of herring fishing on Loch Gilp, with a wooden pier stretched across the bay, but the fish mysteriously vanished before World War I. Mills and dyeworks followed their example, and, besides tourism and Highbank Pottery, where you can see porcelain being made, the main employer is now Argyll and Bute District Council, which has its headquarters at Kilmory Castle.

The castle gardens, open to the public, were partly laid out by Joseph Hooker, first director of Kew Gardens. They are full of rare rhododendrons, and so is Crarae Garden, on the Inveraray road, planted round a spectacular gorge. A little further on is Auchindrain Township, a former working farm which now gives visitors an experience of Highland life. Its houses have period furnishings and the barns are equipped with old implements.

LOCH LOMOND   Strathclyde/Central

Loch Lomond has two distinct characters – the narrow upper loch is hemmed in by mountains, and stretches up into the heart of the Highlands, while the broad, island-speckled southern end is bordered by fertile farmland. Here, within easy reach of Glasgow, are some of Loch Lomond's most popular attractions.

Balloch, with its modern castle, country park and opportunities for boat cruises, sits astride the only natural outlet from the loch, and is a busy centre. Up the west side, off the well-used A82, is Luss, a smart estate village, setting for the television series, *Take the High Road*. Lomond's east side is quieter, and provides greater opportunities for walking and outdoor pursuits. From Balmaha there are good views over some of the loch's 38 named islands – especially Inchcailloch, once the site of a nunnery, and now part of the Loch Lomond National Nature Reserve.

Much of the eastern shore is within the 50,000-acre Queen Elizabeth Forest Park. The road ends at Rowardennan, from where there is a stiff climb up the 3,192 feet (972.9 metres) of Ben Lomond. If you want to visit beautiful Inversnaid, you have to approach from Aberfoyle or by ferry from Inveruglas – unless you are energetic enough for the walk along the West Highland Way from Rowardennan.

THE WEST HIGHLAND WAY

It is on the shores of Loch Lomond that the 95-mile (152.9-km) West Highland Way, Scotland's first long-distance footpath, makes the transition from easy lowland walking to the more rugged terrain of the Highlands. Starting from Milngavie on the outskirts of Glasgow, the route makes its way north to Fort William, often using ancient and historic routes – drove roads by which cattle dealers reached market (like the Devil's Staircase out of Glen Coe), military roads instituted by General Wade to aid in suppressing the clans, old coaching roads and even disused railway lines. Walk all the way if you wish – experts recommend going south to north, to build up stamina for the hills – or take a short walk along the route; there is no shortage of spectacular sections, and you may see red deer and, just possibly, golden eagles on the way.

Loch Lomond is a popular recreation centre within easy reach of Glasgow

There is an old treasure map, now on display at Inveraray Castle, showing the location of the wreck of a Spanish galleon that sank in Tobermory Bay in 1588. After the defeat of the Armada, many Spaniards attempted to get home via the north of Scotland. One such vessel was given supplies by the people of Mull, but the Spanish refused to pay, and even locked up Donald Maclean, who had come to collect the payment. He managed to escape, and blew up the ship, which sank in the bay. Confusion reigns as to whether the ship was a troop carrier, the *San Juan de Sicilia*, or a treasure ship, the *Florida*. Treasure hunters are ever hopeful, and still dive here in search of a shower of golden ducats, yet so far only a few coins and cannon have been raised. Perhaps the crew simply didn't have the means to pay the islanders for their supplies after all.

Brightly painted shops and hotels face on to the sheltered waters of Tobermory Bay

MULL AND IONA   Strathclyde

Take the time to properly explore and discover Mull and you will find it full of interest and beauty. Craignure is the main arrival point, and from Old Pier Station the Mull and West Highland Narrow Gauge Railway runs the extremely scenic 1¼ miles (2 km) to Torosay Castle. This line boasts a real rarity – a new steam locomotive, built in Sheffield in 1993.

Torosay Castle is actually a Victorian mansion, set in 12 acres of superb gardens. The house is full of character and is enthusiastically shared with visitors by its resident owner – you are positively encouraged to sit on chairs, peer into cupboards and browse through the family scrapbooks. Near by, on a craggy point with wonderful views along the Sound of Mull, is 13th-century Duart Castle, centre for the Clan Maclean.

Mountains give way to pastoral scenery on the way to the island's capital, Tobermory, with its houses painted in jolly colours around the bay. Tobermory's tourist attractions – the Mull Museum and the distillery – are diminutive, just like Mull Little Theatre at Dervaig, which is Britain's smallest professional theatre. With just 43 seats, it puts on a summer season with just two or three actors. Calgary, further on, has the best sandy beach on the island.

West of Ben More, Mull's highest mountain, is the Ardmeanach peninsula, the tip of which is only accessible by an arduous 5½-mile (8.8-km) path. Its main sight is a startling fossilised tree, 50 feet (15.2 metres) high and possibly 50 million years old. Boat trips round Mull sometimes give passengers a view of it.

Mull's main road, mostly single-track, traverses the moorland from the east coast to Loch Scridain and on across the Ross of Mull to Fionnphort, for the Iona ferry. South of the road is walking country, with a coastline of basaltic stacks and sea arches – wild and lonely, but full of beauty and fascinating wildlife.

Iona is a magical place. Most visitors make straight for the abbey, but you should spare time for the remains of the 13th-century priory, built for Augustinian nuns. St Columba founded his monastery in 563AD where the abbey now stands, and from it the light of Christianity radiated throughout Europe – the Book of Kells, now on show in Dublin's Trinity College Library, was illuminated here. Columba's foundation ended in 803AD when Vikings slew 68 monks at Martyr's Bay. Later a church and buildings erected by 12th-century Benedictine monks were left in ruins after the Reformation, until restoration began in 1910. Now the home of the Iona Community, founded in 1938, the abbey welcomes pilgrims from around the world. Beside it is the ancient burial ground of the Scottish kings, among them Macbeth and Duncan. The abbey does get busy with visitors at times, but even though the island is small, it is possible to quickly escape the crowds and enjoy the fine sands and rocky landscape, the wild flowers and birds, and the view of the busy world beyond Iona.

Many visitors will approach Staffa humming Mendelssohn's 'Fingal's Cave' Overture. He came to this extraordinary island in 1829, to visit the huge cavern on its south side. Here the volcanic basalt has cooled into its characteristic six-sided columns, making it look like a massive cathedral organ. Cathedral-like, too, is the enormous interior of Fingal's Cave; weather permitting, visitors are allowed to land from some of the many boat trips in the area.

The peaceful island of Iona has for centuries offered a religious retreat

DR JOHNSON ON IONA
Dr Samuel Johnson was not known for his love of things Scottish ('...the noblest prospect which a Scotchman ever sees, is the high road that leads him to England'), but even he was impressed by Iona. He arrived with Boswell on the evening of 19th October 1773 and spent the night, quite comfortably, in a barn. Next day they visited the priory – the nun's church was full of cow dung – and the abbey 'which is really grand enough when one thinks of its antiquity and the remoteness of the place', wrote Boswell. Johnson concurred. 'That man is little to be envied,' he said, 'whose piety would not grow warmer among the ruins of Iona.'

Dun Ara Fort, The Island of Mull

This island walk includes two castles, a group of standing stones and the beautiful coastal scenery of northern Mull. An easy linear walk, with some scrambling on to one of the vertical circular outcrops which are such a feature of northern Mull.

Time: 2 hours. Distance: 3½ miles (5.6 km).
Location: 3½ miles (5.6 km) west of Tobermory.
Start: From Main Street in Tobermory, drive up to Argyll Terrace, following signs for the B882 to Dervaig. After half a mile (0.8 km), at a three-way junction, turn right, signposted 'Glengorm 4 miles', and continue, passing the wireless station. Just before the cattle grid and bridge, pull into the left and park. (OS grid ref: NM447567.)
OS Maps: Landranger 47 (Tobermory and North Mull) 1:50,000.
Pathfinder 302 (Tobermory [Sheet NM 45/55]) 1:25,000.
See Key to Walks on page 121.

ROUTE DIRECTIONS

Walk across the cattle grid and past the farm at Sorne, following the road right. After 200 yards (183 metres), take the left-hand fork up an unmetalled road, marked 'No Cars Please'. Continue up this forested road, past the rhododendrons and fuchsias on the right, until you see **Glengorm Castle**, with its walled vegetable garden and greenhouse.

Turn left and go through the gate at the two slatted barns, turning sharp right downhill through a short wooded section, passing through two more gates. The vista opens up and the road divides. Follow the path that leads straight on uphill. After 100 yards (91 metres) you will see three **standing stones** to the left below the path. Go down to explore.

Return to the path and continue to the brow of the hill. Cross a stile and walk along the left-hand side of a low-lying dry-stone wall, heading down towards the coast. At the foot of the field squeeze past the fence, veer to the left around the foot of the bluff and follow the wide grassy track down to the coast.

The path snakes down to a long stone wall on the left, which turns at right angles near a river bend. Here there are loose boulders on the ground. Look towards the free-standing bluff nearest to the sea, noting the weathered sign at the foot of the cliff. On reaching the sign, scramble up through a narrow gulley on to the flat top of the outcrop (take care in wet weather). Here the foundations of **Dun Ara Fort** can be seen, as well as spectacular views of the coastline, outbuildings of the fort and ancient terracing.

There are many coastal features around the seaward base of the fort to explore. Return to the start point by retracing your steps, with dramatic changes of scenery as you head back inland.

POINTS OF INTEREST

Glengorm Castle
The castle was built in 1860 for James Forsyth, the laird of the Dervaig Clearances, who asked a local woman for advice on what he should call his new home. 'Call the place Glengorm', she replied. Little did he realise that the meaning in Gaelic, 'Blue Glen', was a reference to the Clearances on Mull, when blue smoke raged from the burning homes of entire communities who had been thrown off their land. Glengorm was used as a base for sporting activities in the late 19th century and today is the most important location for the cultivation of vegetables on the island. It is privately owned.

Standing Stones
Mull has one stone circle, 14 settings and 13 single standing stones. The three standing stones, in a circle of boulders, that are to be found on this walk may not have been for sun or moon worship, as is so often assumed, but to establish a fixed calendar for agricultural activities – vital in ancient communities.

Dun Ara Fort
Dun Ara is one of four medieval forts on Mull, and the ruined walls are all that remain of its original three buildings. They are perched on the summit of a small plateau of Tertiary basalt lava close to Sorne Point, with further outbuildings

and signs of ancient cultivation below. The fort is believed to have been a stronghold of the Clan MacKinnon.

Looking out to the rugged Ardnamurchan peninsula from Dun Ara

Around the Isle of Mull

A clockwise island drive of 75 miles (120 km), which takes in interesting geological features, an important mausoleum and an unusual church tower. It is an ideal day trip from Oban on the Scottish mainland in the summer months, or include an overnight stop at Tobermory, the island's main town.

ROUTE DIRECTIONS

See Key to Car Tours on page 120.
From the ferry terminal turn left on to the A849, which soon becomes a single-track road with passing places.
Torosay Castle and

Gardens and **Isle of Mull Weavers** are signed to the left; to visit them, take this turn, the weavers are near by, the castle is straight ahead. The formality of both the castle, designed by the Victorian architect David Bryce, and the

order of the terraced gardens, attributed to Sir Robert Lorimer, contrast strongly with this wild mountainous island. The 12-acre gardens have an Italian statue walk, water garden, rockery and Japanese garden. In the nearby weaving workshop you will find Bob and Kathie Ryan who use old dobby looms to make their own tweeds and tartans.

Return to the A849, turn left and continue to the signpost for Kilpatrick, where you can take a detour to Duart Castle (the name means Dark Headland), one of the oldest inhabited castles in Scotland. Home of the 28th Chief of Clan Maclean, the castle has a keep which dates from 1360.

Continue on the A849 for

beautiful vistas over Loch Don, a shallow sea loch with swans and other waterfowl. Pass the Old Mill Cottage Restaurant and continue towards Loch Spelve with its mussel farm, otters and bird-life. The road bears right inland, passing through mountains and the glen. At the junction signed 'Lochbuie and Croggan' is a squat stone cairn to the Gaelic bard Dughall an-t-Srth-Chaoil (Dugald MacPhail). Continue on the A849 driving through the forest on to open hillsides towards Glen More, with its waterslides and crescent of four small lochs in the valley below – the largest is Loch Airdeglais. Entering the broad treeless valley of Glen More you pass through the central crater of an extinct volcano, six miles (9.6 km) in diameter. Descend to Loch Scridain, turn right at the junction on to the B8035 signed 'Salen'. If you want to take a detour to Iona continue on the A849 to the jetty at Fionnphort.

Continue on the main drive on the B8035, passing Loch Scridain on the left. The road turns inland climbing up through the tree line to the top of the hill, with views across to Dutchman's Cap and Staffa. The road then descends to Loch na Keal and Inch Kenneth and passes waterfalls above the road at Balnahard. Head along the narrow coastal road, with the island of Eorsa on the left, and continue over a hump-backed bridge. The road flattens out and passes over a series of small bridges. At the head of Loch na Keal the road passes through an avenue of rhodo-dendrons by Knock Farm. Cross the River Ba and turn right to Gruline Home Farm to visit the **Macquarie Mausoleum**. Here lie the remains of Lachlan Macquarie (1762–1824), soldier, admin-istrator and Governor of New South Wales. Known as the 'Father of Australia', he was noted for his reformist policies towards ex-convicts and for his record in public works. Macquarie was born on the nearby island of Ulva.

Return to the road and take the B8073, signposted 'Ulva Ferry, Calgary, Dervaig,

The narrow road passes along the shore of Loch na Keal

Tobermory', which rises up to wonderful views of the coastal islands including Ulva. The road passes Eorsa Island again and to the left is a magnifi-cent view of Ben More, which, at 3,171 feet (967 metres), is the only Munro (mountain peak over 3,000 feet/914.4 metres) on Mull. Pass the Sound of Ulva and continue on to Loch Tuath and the spectacular **Eas Fors water-fall**. Continue until you reach Calgary Bay with its beautiful white sandy beach, then carry on to Dervaig. Built in 1799 by MacLean of Coll, the vil-lage has distinct pairs of hous-es which have access to com-mon hill grazing. Kilmore church has an unusual slim Irish-style round tower.

Stay on the B8073, which ascends passing numerous lochs, including Loch Frisa, until you arrive in Tobermory. If you wish to take the ferry back to the mainland turn right on to the A848 and drive to Craignure.

FERRY CONVENIENT

You can't get far in Western Scotland without needing to catch a ferry, especially to its 130 or so inhabited islands. Many of the shorter routes are operated by local owners and provide an excellent service, but Caledonian MacBrayne – CalMac – is undoubtedly the name you will come across most. The company was formed in 1973 when MacBraynes, operators of shipping services, mostly to the Western Isles, since 1851, joined forces with the Clyde-based Caledonian Steam Packet Company, a youngster from 1889. CalMac sails to 23 islands and operates more than 30 ferries in a huge range of sizes, from the largest vessel on the Ullapool to Stornoway route to the tiny four-car ferry that plies between Tarbert at the top of Kintyre and Portavadie.

The view from MacCaig's Folly across Oban to the islands is spectacular

OBAN Strathclyde Map ref NM8629

To experience the true splendour of Oban, you should climb at dusk to MacCaig's improbable Gothic Coliseum and watch the glorious sunset over the Firth of Lorn and the mountains of Morvern and Mull. MacCaig, 'Art Critic, Philosophical Essayist and Banker' of Oban, engaged unemployed stonemasons on his spectacular tower from around 1897, and though it was never finished, it is Oban's most notable landmark. At its foot, the bay, sheltered by Kerrera Island, is always busy with pleasure craft.

Much of the harbour front is dominated by hotels, and ferries for the Hebrides depart from Railway Quay. Here, too, is the Oban Glass Studio where you can see the creation of jewel-like paperweights, and buy them, of course. Oban Distillery, in the heart of the town, welcomes visitors, and near by, on North Pier, is A World In Miniature, with perfectly detailed, small-scale displays of rooms and tiny furniture.

Northwards, the fine tower of St Columba's Cathedral dominates the bay, and beyond it are the remains of Dunollie Castle, seat of the MacDougall Lords of Lorne. Further afield, Dunstaffnage Castle is worth visiting. This ruined stronghold, with gatehouse, two round towers and 10-foot (3-metre) thick walls, stands on a rocky outcrop at the mouth of Loch Etive, and was once the prison of Flora Macdonald.

Across the Connel Bridge at Barcaldine is the Sea Life Centre, with its close-up – and even hands-on – displays of British marine life. Equally fishy is the Scottish Salmon and Seafood Centre, where you can find out all about fish farms and, of course, sample their product. And don't miss Arduaine Garden with its superb collection of rhododendrons and wonderful views.

Argyll and Kintyre

Leisure Information

Places of Interest

Shopping

The Performing Arts

Sports, Activities

and the Outdoors

Annual Events and Customs

Checklist

Leisure Information

TOURIST INFORMATION CENTRES

Ballachulish
(Seasonal). Tel: 01855 811296.
Bowmore
Islay. Tel: 01496 810254.
Campbeltown
Mackinnon House, The Pier. Tel:
01586 552056.
Craignure
(Seasonal). Tel: 01680 812377.
Dunoon
7 Alexandra.Parade. Tel: 01369
703785.
Inveraray
Front Street. Tel: 01499 302063.
Kilchoan
Ardnamurchan (seasonal). Tel:
01972 510222.
Lochgilphead
(Seasonal). Tel: 01546 602344.
Oban
Argyll Square. Tel: 01631
563122.
Strontian
(Seasonal). Tel: 01967 402131.
Tarbert
Harbour Street (seasonal). Tel:
01880 820429.
Tobermory
Mull. Tel: 01688 302182.

OTHER INFORMATION

Ferries
Caledonian MacBrayne Ferries.

Ferry Terminal, Gourock. Tel:
01475 650100. For Hebrides via
Firth of Clyde and west coast
ports; sailings to 23 islands.
'Rover' tickets available.
Western Ferries (Clyde) 61
Woodside Crescent, Glasgow.
Tel: 0141 332 9766.
Forest Enterprise
Forestry Commision, 231
Corstorphine Road, Edinburgh.
Tel: 0131 334 0303.
Historic Scotland
Longmore House, Salisbury
Place, Edinburgh. Tel: 0131 668
8800.
National Trust for Scotland
5 Charlotte Square, Edinburgh.
Tel: 0131 226 5922.
**Royal Society for the
Protection of Birds**
17 Regent Terrace, Edinburgh.
Tel: 0131 556 5624.
Scottish Tourist Board
23 Ravelston Terrace,
Edinburgh. Tel: 0131 332 2433.
Scottish Wildlife Trust
16 Cramond Glebe Road,
Edinburgh. Tel: 0131 312 7765.
Weather
Great Outdoors Weatherline.
Tel: 0891 567538. Mountaincall
for north-west Scotland. Tel:
0891 505680. Western
Highlands, Climbing line. Tel:
0891 200819. Weathercall for
north-west Scotland. Tel: 0891
500425.

ORDNANCE SURVEY MAPS

Landranger 1:50,000 sheet
numbers 47, 48, 49, 50, 55, 56,
60, 61, 62, 63, 68, 69.

Places of Interest

There will be an admission
charge at the following places of
interest unless otherwise stated.
Achamore House Gardens
Gigha, via ferry from Tayinloan.
Tel: 01583 505267/505254.
Open: all year, daily.
Arctic Penguin
The Harbour, Inveraray. Tel:
01499 302213. Open: all year
daily except Christmas and New
Year's Day.
Ardanaiseig Gardens
Four miles (6.4 km) north east of
Kilchrenan. Tel: 01866 833333.
Open: end Mar–Oct daily.
Arduaine Garden
On A816 20 miles (32.2 km)
south of Oban. Tel: 01852
200366. Open: all year daily.
**Auchindrain Township
Open-Air Museum**
On A83, 5½ miles (8.8 km) south
west of Inveraray. Tel: 01499
500235. Open: Apr–Sep most
days.
Balloch Castle Country Park
Balloch. Tel: 01389 758216.
Open: Apr–Sep daily.
Boathouse Visitor Centre
Isle of Mull. (Ulva Ferry–by Aros)

8 miles (12.8 km) west of Salen on the B8035 and B8073. Tel: 01688 500264/500266. Open: mid Apr–mid Oct most days.

Bonawe Iron Furnace
Taynuilt. 12 miles (19.2 km) east of Oban on A85. Tel: 01866 822432. Open: Apr–Sep most days.

Carnasserie Castle
Two miles (3.2 km) north of Kilmartin, off A816. Tel: 0131 668 8800. Open: all reasonable times. Free.

Crarae Glen Garden
Minard. Tel: 01546 886614. Open: all year daily; visitor centre Easter–Oct.

Duart Castle
Isle of Mull. Tel: 01680 812309. Open: May–mid Oct daily. Grounds free.

Dunstaffnage Castle and Chapel
4 miles (6.4 km) north of Oban, off A85. Tel: 0131 668 8800. Open: Apr–Sep most days.

Grogport Organic Tannery
Grogport Old Manse. 4 miles (6.4 km) north of Carradale. Tel: 01583 431255. Open: all reasonable times. Free.

Inveraray Castle
Half a mile (0.8 km) north of Inveraray. Tel: 01499 302203. Open: Apr–Oct most days.

Inveraray Jail
Church Square, Inveraray. Tel: 01499 302381. Open: all year daily except Christmas Day and New Year's Day.

Kilmun Hill: Arboretum and Forest Walks
Kilmun. Five miles (8 km) north of Dunoon on A880, one mile (1.6 km) east of junction with A815. Tel: 01369 840666. Open: all year daily. Free.

Mull Museum
Main Street, Tobermory, Isle of Mull. Open: Easter–mid Oct most days.

Torosay Castle and Gardens
Mull. One mile (1.6 km) south of Craignure. Tel: 01680 812421. Open: Easter, then mid Apr–mid Oct daily. Gardens all year daily.

Younger Botanic Garden
Benmore. Seven miles (11.2 km) north of Dunoon on A815. Tel: 01369 706261. Open: mid Mar–Oct daily.

SPECIAL INTEREST FOR CHILDREN

The following places may be of interest to visitors with children. Unless otherwise stated there will be an admission charge.

Argyll Wildlife Park
Dalchenna, 2 miles (3.2 km) south west of Inveraray. Tel: 01499 302264. Open: Mar–Dec daily.

Cowal Bird Garden
Lochan Wood, Dunoon. On A885. Tel: 01369 840219. Open: Apr–Nov daily.

Glenfinart Deer Farm
Barnacabber Farm, half a mile (0.8 km) north of Ardentinny. Tel: 0136 981 331. Open: Easter–Oct; Nov–Easter by appointment.

Holy Loch Farm Park and Highland Cattle Centre
Dalinlongart, Sandbank. On A815, 4 miles (6.4 km) north of Dunoon. Tel: 01369 706429. Open: Apr–Oct daily.

Oban Rare Breeds Farm
New Barran, 2 miles (3.2 km) east of Oban on the Glencruitten road. Tel: 01631 775608. Open: late Mar–late Oct, daily.

Sea Life Centre
Barcaldine, on A828, 10 miles (16.1 km) north east of Oban off A828. Tel: 01631 723826. Open: mid Feb–Nov daily; weekends only in winter.

A World in Miniature
North Pier, Oban. Tel: 01852 316272. Open: Easter–Oct daily.

Shopping

LOCAL SPECIALITIES

Distilleries
Bowmore Distillery, Bowmore. Tel: 01496 810441. Open: all year most days. Bunnahabhain Distillery, Port Askaig. Tel: 01496 840646. Open: all year most days. Caol Ila Distillery, Port Askaig. Tel: 01496 840207 (appointment only). Lagavulin Distillery, Port Ellen. Tel: 01496 302400 (appointment only). Laphroaig Distillery, Port Ellen. Tel: 01496 302418 (appointment only). Oban Distillery, Stafford Street, Oban. Tel: 01631 564262. Open: all year weekdays only.

Food
Scottish Salmon and Seafood Centre, 6 miles (9.6 km) south of Oban on A816. Tel: 01852 316263. Open: daily. Inverawe Smokery, Bridge of Awe, near Taynuilt, 2 miles (3.2 km) off A85 Oban to Glasgow road. Tel: 01866 822446. Open: all year daily.

Glass
Oban Glass Studio, Heritage Wharf, Railway Pier, Oban. Tel: 01631 563386.

Pottery
Dunoon Ceramics, Hamilton Street, Dunoon. Tel: 01369 704360. Highland Porcelain Pottery, Lochgilphead. Tel: 01546 602044.

The Performing Arts

Highland Theatre
George Street, Oban. Tel: 01631 562444.

Mull Little Theatre
Dervaig, Isle of Mull. Tel: 01684 250/01688 302062.

Sports, Activities and the Outdoors

ANGLING

There are ample opportunities for angling of all kinds in the area. Enquire at local Tourist Information Offices.

BEACHES

There are lots of lovely sandy beaches all around this area. Calgary, Carradale and Kiloran Bay are particularly good

BOAT TRIPS

Loch Awe
Tel: 0141 334 2529/0183 82440.

Loch Craignish
At Ardfern Yacht Centre between Oban and Lochgilphead. Take B8002 off the A816. Contact Kingfisher Cruises, tel: 01852 500662.

Loch Etive
Connel Bridge, 12 miles (19.2 km) east of Oban on A85 (signposted). Free transport for walkers from Taynuilt. Tel: 01866 822430.

COUNTRY PARKS, FORESTS AND NATURE RESERVES

Argyll Forest Park
Access from: A83, B828, B839 and A815. Guided walks in summer. Tel: 01369 840666.

Glen Nant Forest Nature Reserve
Two miles (3.2 km) south of Taynuilt on B845. Tel: 01631 566155.

CYCLING

Argyll Forest Park
Waymarked cycling routes. Contact Forest Enterprise, Kilmun by Dunoon, Argyll. Tel: 01369 840666.

Crinan Canal towpath (Ardrishaig to Crinan)
Contact Canal Office Pier Square, Ardrishaig. Tel: 01546 3210. Lorne Forest Enterprise, Oban. Tel: 01631 566155.

Lauder Forest Walks
Glenbranter Estate, 3 miles (4.8 km) south of Strachur on A815 (signposted).

CYCLE HIRE

Ballachulish
Mountain Madness, Albert Road, Ballachulish. Tel: 01855 811728.

Lochgilphead
Barmollock Farm, Kilmichael Glen, near Ford. Tel: 01546 810209.
Crinan Cycles, Pier workshop, Chalmers Street, Ardrishaig. Tel: 01546 603511.

GOLF COURSES

Craignure (Mull)
Craignure Golf Club, 1 mile (1.6 km) north of Craignure. Tel: 01680 812370.

Dalmally
Dalmally Golf Club, Old Saw Mill. Tel: 01838 200281.

Dunoon
Cowal Golf Club, off A815 at Kirn. Tel: 01369 702216.

Machrihanish
Machrihanish Golf Club. Tel: 01586 810213.

Oban
Glencruitten Golf Club, Glencruitten Road, 1 mile (1.6 km) from town centre, follow signs for Rare Breeds Farm. Tel: 01631 562868/ 564115.

Port Ellen (Islay)
Machrie Hotel, 3 miles (4.8 km) north of Port Ellen. Tel: 01496 302409.

Scalasaig (Colonsay)
Colonsay Golf Club, 2 miles (3.2 km) west of Scalasaig Harbour. Tel: 01951 200316.

Tarbert
Tarbert Golf Club,1 mile (1.6 km) south at head of West Loch Tarbert. Tel: 01880 820536.

Tighnabruaich
Kyles of Bute Golf Club. Tel: 01700 811550.

Tobermory (Mull)
Tobermory Golf Club, half a mile (0.8 km) north off A848. Tel: 01688 2012.

HORSE-RIDING

Aros (Mull)
Lochside Ponies, Crannich, Aros. Tel: 01688 500206.

Dunoon
Velvet Path Riding and Trekking Centre, Innellan by Dunoon. Tel: 01369 830580.

Lochgilphead
Castle Riding Centre, Brenfield, Ardrishaig. Tel: 01546 603274.

Oban
Melfort Riding Centre, Kilmelford by Oban. Tel: 01852 200257.

Port Ellen (Islay)
Ballivicar Farm, (trekking). Tel: 01496 302251. Rockside Farm Riding Centre, Bruichladdich. Tel: 01496 850231.

LONG-DISTANCE FOOTPATHS AND TRAILS

Lauder Forest Walks
Glenbranter Estate, 3 miles (4.8 km) south of Strachur on A815 (signposted).

Puck's Glen
A815, 5 miles (8 km) west of Dunoon in Argyll Forest Park.

West Highland Way
A 95-mile (152.9-km) walk from Milngavie to Fort William.

SAILING

Appin
Linnhe Marine Watersports Centre. Tel: 01631 730227.

Lochgilphead
Argyll Isles Cruising Tuition. Tel: 01546 602670.

Oban
Oban Sea School. Tel: 016315 62013.

Tighnabruaich
Tighnabruaich Sailing School. Tel: 01700 811396.

SEAPLANE TRIPS

Corryvreckan Whirlpool
Contact Tourist Information Offices for information.

WATERSPORTS

Appin
Linnhe Marine Watersports Centre (waterskiing, windsurfing). Tel: 01631 730227.

Carradale
Carradale Canoe Centre, Mull of Kintyre. Tel: 01583 431610.

Glencoe
Glencoe Outdoor Centre (windsurfing). Tel: 01855 811350.

Mallaig
Minch Charters, Harbour Slipway. Tel: 01687 462304/ 462378.

Oban
Puffin Dive Centre, Gallanach (sub aqua). Tel: 01631 566088.

Annual Events and Customs

Dunoon
Cowal Highland Gathering, late August.

Inveraray
Inveraray Traditional Highland Games, mid July.

Machrihanish
Machrihanish Surf Rodeo, mid August.

Oban
Kilmore and Kilbride Highland Games, mid June.
Argyllshire Highland Gathering, late August.

Taynuilt
Taynuilt Highland Games, late July.

Tobermory (Mull)
Tour of Mull Car Rally, early to mid October.

The checklists give details of just some of the facilities within the area covered by this guide. Further information can be obtained from Tourist Information Centres.

Inverness

Superlatives become quite commonplace in the Inverness district, which includes Britain's deepest area of fresh water, Loch Ness, and the highest mountain, Ben Nevis (4,406 feet/1,343 metres). In this area you will also find the most Arctic environment in Britain – on the plateau surrounding Ben Macdhui on the high tops of the Cairngorms. The Great Glen, a dramatic geological fault, slices Scotland in two, creating an exceptional landscape, and at its north-eastern extremity is the town of Inverness, the 'Capital of the Highlands'. Here, too, are the mysteries of Loch Ness, the optimism of Glenfinnan, the bloody deeds of Glen Coe and the tragedy of Culloden.

LANGUAGE OF THE LAND
In Scotland lakes are lochs, and 'ben' means mountain. Like many Highland placenames, these are Gaelic words, and often give an idea of the kind of place they refer to – 'kin' (Gaelic *ceann*), for example, means head, so Kinloch means the top of a lake, while 'inver' (*inbhir*) denotes an outlet – Inverness is where the River Ness meets the sea. 'Tarbert' (or 'Tarbet') means isthmus or crossing place. Other pointers include 'ard', a height, 'ban' meaning white; 'beg', confusingly meaning little, and 'more', meaning great. It all adds another dimension to the landscape.

The red sandstone Glenborrodale Castle Hotel is superbly set above the bay

ARDNAMURCHAN AND MORVERN Highland
You can go no further west on mainland Britain than Ardnamurchan Point, with its spectacular views over to Mull, Coll and Tiree. The whole peninsula, with its rocky hills and desolate moorland, gale-blown trees and heather-capped promontories, has an 'end-of-the-world' feeling. The main road mostly hugs the northern shore of Loch Sunart, rich in birdlife, and you can take a minor road to Ardnamurchan's north coast as the main road passes round Beinn nan Losgann, or continue to the crofting village of Kilchoan, with its ferry to Tobermory. The 13th-century Mingarry Castle, built on its sheer cliff to guard the entrance to Loch Sunart, is where James IV accepted the submission of the Lord of the Isles in 1495; Hanoverian troops built barracks inside it 350 years later. Make a detour to Sanna Bay for views to Muck, Rum and Canna and for superb wildflowers by the beach.

Morvern, across Loch Sunart, is a rugged land with gentler green glens. Lochaline, a popular yachting haven, is reached either by road along Glen Gleann, or by ferry from Mull. There are two castles in the area – the remains of Ardtornish, east of the village, and well-preserved Kinlochailine at the head of Loch Aline. The silica sands at Lochaline have been quarried commercially for manufacturing optical glass. Fiunary, along the Sound of Mull, was the birthplace of George Macleod, founder of the Iona Community. Caisteal nan Con is a small fortress guarding the Sound of Mull. The road ends four miles (6.4 km) beyond, near Drimnin, with views towards Tobermory.

CANNICH   Highland Map ref NH3331

The broad Strath Glass from the north leads to the modern village of Cannich where four valleys meet. Eastwards, down Glen Urquhart, is the prehistoric Corrimony Cairn, still with its stone roof and eleven standing stones. Glen Cannich is entered by a winding road between bare mountain tops, with groves of birch and alder. It widens towards Loch Mullardoch – its dam, at 2,385 feet (726.5 metres), is the longest in Scotland.

The approach to Glen Affric, perhaps the most beautiful of Scottish valleys, passes the popular Dog Falls. Along the 6 miles (9.7 km) of Loch Beinn a'Mheadhoin are parking spots, many with fine walks from them. On the opposite side is one of the largest remnants of the ancient Caledonian Pine Forest, fenced to keep out deer and allow regeneration. Beyond the loch the road ends, but you can walk on to Loch Affric – a magical scene of clustered hills, birch and pine forest; in the autumn there is dazzling colour and the hint of snow on the peaks. You can follow the old track through the mountains to Sheil Bridge in Kintail.

Loch Beinn a'Mheadhoin lies in the lovely setting of Glen Affric

ATTAINING THE HEIGHTS
Until well into the 19th century everyone thought that Ben Macdhui in the Cairngorms, and not Ben Nevis, was Britain's highest mountain. It was the peak everyone climbed, including Gladstone and even Queen Victoria. She wrote in her journal, 'Nothing could be grander or wilder; the rocks are so grand and precipitous, and the snow on Ben Macdhui has such fine effect.' Like Everest, only recognised as the world's highest mountain in the 19th century, Ben Nevis remained unrecognised until accurate measurement was made by the Ordnance Survey in 1846 and the issue was resolved – Ben Nevis is the highest at 4,406 feet (1,343 metres), and Ben Macdhui is runner up at 4,296 feet (1,309 metres).

Lochan Mor and Loch an Eilein

A pleasant walk through the ancient Caledonian pinewoods of the Rothiemurchus Estate, passing three unique lochs and an island castle. It is a level walk, on well-marked paths, which can be shortened if required.

Time: 4 hours. Distance: 7½ miles (12.1 km).
Location: At Inverdruie, 1 mile (1.6 km) south of Aviemore on the B970.
Start: From Aviemore take the B970 south to Inverdruie and park at the Rothiemurchus Visitor Centre.
(OS grid ref: NH902110.)
OS Maps: Landranger 36 (Grantown, Aviemore & Cairngorms area) 1:50,000.
Outdoor Leisure 3 (Aviemore & the Cairngorms) 1:25,000.
See Key to Walks on page 121.

ROUTE DIRECTIONS

From the car park at the Visitor Centre cross the B970 to the village green, walk across the green veering to the left and cross the next road. Go through the gate to the Rothiemurchus footpath in the wood. Head uphill through the wood and over a stile on to open moorland. After crossing a second stile continue on into the forest, keeping right. Just before the brow of the second hill take a small path on the right to two lochans.

Return to the original path and continue to the ridge above **Lochan Mor**, renowned for its waterlilies. Return to the path, turn left and continue to Milton Cottage. From the cottage take the metalled road to the Loch an Eilein car park, fork right and go over the wooden footbridge. The Information Centre and lime kiln are on your right. After 20 yards (18 metres) ascend to the left into the trees and down to the path along the shore of **Loch an Eilein** with its ruined castle.

Continue uphill to the pink granite memorial to Major General Walter Brook Rice, who drowned here while skating on thin ice on Boxing Day 1892. Leave the lake and turn right to return to the main path at Loch an Eilein Cottage. Turn left into the **Caledonian Pine Forest** and follow the white footpath arrow pointing left at the end of the loch. After 500 yards (457 metres) turn right on to the path which leads down to Loch Gamhna; for good views of the loch turn left after 50 yards (46 metres).

Return to the main path, continue and pass a cairn on the left. Turn sharp right over the footbridge for a second view of Loch Gamhna. Return to the main path and keep straight ahead, ignoring the track to the right, and cross the ford into pine forest. Continue straight on and follow the sign to Aviemore; do not take the Lairig Ghru drovers' road. Cross the footbridge over the stream and continue, passing through the wooden swing gate. Leave Loch an Eilein on the metalled road, fork immediately right uphill at the

Loch an Eilein Castle was a stronghold of the Anglo-Norman Comyn family

distinctive triangle of grass, pass through a swing gate on to a rising path, go over a stile and pass a farmhouse and ruined buildings. Keep on, between two white buildings (the left one 'Blackpark'), and through an open fence. The road becomes metalled at this point. Carry on for 100 yards (91 metres) until you intersect the footpath which crosses the road. At the iron gate turn left on to the path signed 'Rothiemurchus footpath'. Continue and turn right to rejoin the original path from the Visitors' Centre and return to the car park.

POINTS OF INTEREST

Lochan Mor
This calm glacial lochan is particularly beautiful in the summer when its lily pads and flowers are at their best, and in the autumn when the birch trees change colour.

Loch an Eilein
Translated as the 'Loch of the Island' and famous for its ruined castle, there are also connections with the infamous Alexander Stewart (1343–1405) – 'The Wolf of Badenoch'. Grandson of Robert the Bruce, he earned his nickname by the razing of Forres and the burning of Elgin Cathedral.

Caledonian Pine Forest
The Great Caledonian Forest once covered all but the mountain tops of Scotland to a height of 2,500 feet (762 metres). Today the timberline is mostly found at 2,000 feet (610 metres). Pinewoods throughout Scotland have been destroyed since medieval times to make way for sheep, and when this became less profitable, deer stalking and grouse shooting took over. Rothiemurchus Forest (translated from Gaelic as 'the plain of the great pine') is a rare survivor, giving some idea of what the native Scottish landscape once looked like.

EARLY CAIRNS

If you think archaeological sites are dull, visit the fascinating Clava Cairns near Culloden, which opens a window on our remote ancestors. A site of major archaeological importance, and very beautifully set among beech trees, it has three large stone burial mounds, each surrounded by a circle of standing stones. They were probably built between about 2000 and 1500BC. The two outer cairns, partly covered in small boulders, have stone-lined passages to the centre. The middle one is hollow, though with no passage. Instead, it has rough cobbled pavements leading away from it. Clava Cairns is part of a whole series of such monuments found only in the region of the Moray Firth.

A simple stone marks the spot where the Stewarts of Appin fell in battle at Culloden

CULLODEN   Highland Map ref NH7246

The Battle of Culloden marked the end of the Stuart ambition to regain the throne of Britain from the Hanoverians. On this bleak and desolate moorland east of Inverness, 5,000 Highlanders under the command of The Young Pretender – Bonnie Prince Charlie – faced 9,000 troops led by the Duke of Cumberland. It was 16th April 1746, a day of bitter cold, with snow flurries. The Highlanders, used to short skirmishes, were no match for the disciplined and well-armed soldiers, and despite courageous fighting were swiftly defeated. Cumberland ordered that no prisoners should be taken; all were killed, earning Cumberland his nickname of 'Butcher'.

Although it can be very crowded in summer, Culloden remains a moving place. The 1,200 Highlanders who died were buried in clan graves, marked by small, weathered stones. The 76 English dead lie in The Field of the English. Near by is the Well of the Dead, a spring where drinking Highlanders were killed. Coloured flags fly over the battlefield to mark the disposition of the armies, and the focal point of the area is a large 19th-century memorial cairn, built where the fighting was most ferocious. Old Leonach Cottage, thatched in heather, has been restored to its 18th-century condition; outside the cottage 30 of the Pretender's troops were burned alive.

The Visitor Centre, with an excellent slide presentation, has clear explanations of the battle, its causes and its aftermath. Prince Charles fled to the hills and eventually escaped to France, with Flora Macdonald's help. The clans were ruthlessly suppressed – the kilt, tartan, the Gaelic language and even the bagpipes were proscribed.

FORT WILLIAM Highland Map ref NN1073

Fort William's greatest asset is its close proximity to Ben Nevis, Britain's highest mountain, which stands sentinel over the Nevis range about seven miles (11.3 km) to the north. The town is also at the southern entrance to the Great Glen and at the head of Loch Linnhe, with routes to Badenoch and Skye, but this is not just a place to venture from – it has its own delights too. Treasures of The Earth is a huge collection of rare gemstones, crystals and fossils, including Europe's largest uncut emerald, and visitors can also discover gems of information, such as how amethyst crystals take a quarter of a million years to grow just one inch (5cm). The West Highland Museum, famous for its Jacobite collections, is advertised as 'an old-fashioned museum – it is full of information and full of surprises'.

Until recently the tops of Scotland's mountain ranges were the exclusive preserve of the athletic, but now everyone can experience breathtaking views without so much as getting out of breath. Panoramic vistas to the upper slopes of Aonach Mor (4,000 feet/1,219.2 metres) open up from enclosed gondola cable cars which cover about 1½ miles (2.4 km) in their climb to an altitude of 2,150 feet (655.3 metres). The ascent takes about 15 minutes and at the top, in addition to the views across Loch Lochy, the Great Glen, Loch Eil and the Inner Hebrides, you will find a restaurant, a licensed bar, a sports shop, telescopes, interpretative plaques and slide presentations. There are a number of walks but do keep to the paths, both for your own safety and for conservation. Two recommended walks are to Sgurr Finnisg-aig (about 20 minutes each way) and to Meal Beag (about 30 minutes each way).

The faint lines of the Parallel Roads are a natural feature of Glen Roy

THE PARALLEL ROADS

In a quiet valley 18 miles (29 km) north east of Fort William is a geological phenomenon which is unique in Britain. Glen Roy and its side valleys are marked by three strange parallel lines known as the 'Parallel Roads', not roads at all, but the shorelines of an ancient glacial loch. Towards the end of the last Ice Age, 10,000 years ago, the valley was dammed with ice that melted in three stages, leaving these horizontal ridges along the valley slopes. The Nature Conservancy Council explain it all on an interpretative board above the car park. To get to Glen Roy from Fort William, go north on the A82, turn right on to the A86 at Spean Bridge, then left on an unclassified road at Roy Bridge.

The Water of Nevis

This well-established walk through the Glen Nevis Gorge, past superb waterfalls, takes in magnificent wider vistas, with a view of the summit of Ben Nevis and a ruined shepherd's cottage. A sturdy walk, with some steep and tricky passes, requiring reasonable agility and good footwear.

Time: 4 hours. Distance: 5 miles (8 km).
Location: 5 miles (8 km) south east of Fort William.
Start: Take the A82 Inverness road from Fort William to the roundabout on the outskirts of town; take the second exit signposted 'Glen Nevis'. Drive up the Glen to the end and cross the river past the first car park, and on for a further 1½ miles (2.4 km) and park in the car park at end of the road.
(OS grid ref: NN168691.)
OS Maps: Landranger 41 (Ben Nevis, Fort William & area) 1:50,000.
Pathfinder 290 (Kinlochleven) Sheet NN 06/16 1:25,000.
See Key to Walks on page 121.

ROUTE DIRECTIONS

Follow the path leading from the car park into the boulder-strewn and beautifully wooded Nevis Gorge, signposted 'Corrour/ Rannoch', noting the Sheet Falls cascading down the side of **Ben Nevis** on the left. Continue into the gorge past fallen blocks of pink granite, and ascend through a wooded section stepping over any fords. The path may be slippery at this point, so take care when you need to ford streams or scramble over small rock outcrops, as the drop on the right is severe. The views of the falls on your right and the view back to the Sheet Falls cascading from

The fall of An Steall tumbles into the Water of Nevis amid the dramatic landscape of Glen Nevis

Ben Nevis are outstanding.

At the top of the falls you pass out of the wooded gorge on to a broad flat valley with an upland meadow backed by the **An Steall Falls**. There is a distinct change in atmosphere as the rumble of the falls abates to be replaced by an eerie silence. Keep to the left-hand side of the valley floor. Follow the valley around the bend to the left. After 100 yards (91 metres) step across the river on to the beech bar, and follow the path to the other side of the bar in front of the reed beds.

Walk further into the valley along this side of the river, avoiding any overly muddy sections. Cross the wooden bridge over to the Steall Ruin, once a shepherds' house, and carry on to the white quartzite path ahead which rises to give wonderful views back to the Ben Nevis massif (weather permitting), and the rugged Mamores on your right.

Stop after you reach the third side stream at the final rise in the path. From here there are remarkable vistas in both directions. In the winter deer come down into this valley. Do not venture further, but return by the same route, this time taking in the view of the An Steall Falls, and a look at the three-wire suspension bridge over the river before returning to the car park by the same path.

POINTS OF INTEREST
Ben Nevis
Ben Nevis is the highest mountain in the British Isles, at 4,406 feet (1,343 metres). The name 'Nevis' derives from the Gaelic *neamh*, meaning 'heaven' or 'clouds'. The 'mountain with its head in the clouds' was formed around 350 million years ago through volcanic activity. The five-mile (8-km) track to the top typically takes five to seven hours to climb and descend, that is unless you are extremely athletic. There is an annual hill race here, the fastest time being a staggering 1 hour and 25 minutes. The tourist path up the mountain starts from the Visitor Centre by Achintee House. (OS Map Landranger 41, grid ref:

NN123729). Due to its altitude, the top of Ben Nevis is covered in snow during winter and spring, while its proximity to the sea ensures that cloud covers it for as much as 300 days of the year.

Glen Nevis
Described as one of the best glens in Scotland, and frequently compared with the Himalayas, Glen Nevis has been used as a location for many films, including, most recently, *Rob Roy*. It is in fact a glacial valley carved out during the Great Ice Age, which started two million years ago.

Water of Nevis and An Steall Falls
Many falls rush with terrifying power like a curtain through this dramatic gorge. The Upper Falls of Nevis is, at 350 feet (107 metres), the third highest waterfall in Britain, after Glomach in Wester Ross and Eas Coul Aulin in Sutherland. An Steall Bhan in translation means 'the White Spout'.

GOING DOWNHILL FAST

Glen Coe's skiing may not be as fashionable as Klosters', but it can be just as exciting. From White Corries at the top of the glen, where the fascinating Museum of Scottish Skiing and Mountaineering puts the sport into perspective, a chairlift takes skiers (and summer visitors, too) high into the mountains, with superb views to Rannoch Moor and beyond. There are 15 runs catering for all abilities, some with intriguing names – Fly Paper, for example, and Mug's Alley. Instruction is available, too. If hurtling downhill doesn't appeal, the Glen Coe area offers cross-country skiing, ski mountaineering, speed skating, snowboarding and even paragliding.

Looking down the steep valley of Glen Coe, with the Three Sisters peaks away to the left

GLEN COE AND RANNOCH MOOR   Highland/ Grampian Map ref NN1058/NN3052

On 13 February 1692 the Campbells defied the traditions of Highland hospitality and massacred 38 members of the Macdonald clan in Glen Coe. Alastair Macdonald, like many clansmen reluctant to accept William and Mary as monarchs, failed to get papers attesting his loyalty to a magistrate by the deadline, the end of 1691, though they did arrive in Edinburgh in the new year. However, the papers were suppressed by the Under Secretary of State, who then told Campbell of Glenlyon that the Macdonalds 'must all be slaughtered'. Campbell and his men, pretending to be delayed on a journey, were accommodated by the Macdonalds in Glen Coe for a fortnight, then cold-bloodedly slaughtered their hosts.

The atrocity took place in the lower glen by Glencoe village, where the heather-roofed museum has displays of Highland life. The most dramatic part of Glen Coe is higher up. From the roof of the National Trust for Scotland visitor centre there is a fine view of outstanding mountain scenery of stark peaks and glittering waterfalls. You can find out about the many exhilarating walks from the visitor centre; there is challenging climbing, too, for the experienced.

South west of Glen Coe, Rannoch Moor is a vast expanse of peat bog, treacherous even in the driest season. Rannoch actually means 'watery' in Gaelic. The finest view is perhaps from the railway as it crosses on its way north to Fort William, but the best approach by car is along Loch Rannoch. On its south side is the Black Wood of Rannoch, native Caledonian forest of ancient pines and groves of alder, birch and juniper. Just beyond Bridge of Gaur is a house built as barracks for Hanoverian troops after Culloden – a bleak posting. Rannoch Station is the end of the road, though it is possible to walk from here on old tracks. In places you will come across the blackened stumps of ancient trees protruding from the peat, as evidence that this forlorn place was once covered in forest.

GLENELG   Highland Map ref NG8119

The old military road that leads to Glenelg rockets off the main Kyle of Lochalsh road, climbing rapidly up the Mam Ratagain pass to a viewpoint offering stunning views of the Five Sisters of Kintail above Loch Duich. There follows a gentler descent into Glen More, where a side road goes to the six-car turntable ferry that is a romantic alternative to the new bridge to Skye.

The Glenelg road passes the gaunt remains of Bernera Barracks, built in 1722 for Hanoverian troops. Continue for 2½ miles (4 km) into Glen Beag for Glenelg's most famous sight – its two brochs. The circular walls of Dun Telve still stand to 33 feet (10 metres), and are 13 feet (3.9 metres) wide at the base. Dun Troddan is more ruined, but in both you can still see the remains of the internal galleries and stairways.

Admirers of Gavin Maxwell's *Ring of Bright Water* will want to go further along the coast to Sandaig, where the author lived and kept his famous otters in the 1950s. The house he called Camusfearna in his books stood near the shore of the beautiful bay, but burned down and was demolished, on his orders, after his death. His ashes lie under a boulder here, and there is a cairn with an inscription to Edal the otter.

Beyond Shiel Bridge the road to Glenelg climbs steeply, giving excellent views down Loch Duich towards Eilean Donan Castle

SCOTS BROCHS

Only Scotland has brochs, those distinct, cooling-tower-shaped structures, built in the Iron Age, from around 100BC to 100AD. Some 500 sites have been identified, mostly near the sea and in areas where timber was scarce but stone was plentiful. No one knows what their function was, but they were probably defensive – the name is from Old Norse *borg*, meaning a fortress. The open interiors had galleries and parapets, and elaborate internal staircases, all carefully constructed. The best-preserved is on Mousa in Shetland, with its 40-foot (12.2-metre) walls.

The Glenfinnan Monument is a poignant Jacobite memorial

CONCRETE BOB'S VIADUCT
The West Highland Railway gives wonderful views down Loch Shiel from the Glenfinnan Viaduct, and the viaduct itself is impressive. It was built when the line from Glasgow, which had struggled across Rannoch Moor to Fort William by 1894, was extended to Mallaig in 1902. Curving for 1,000 feet (304.8 metres) over the River Finnan, its 21 huge concrete arches are up to 100 feet (30.5 metres) high. The viaduct was the work of Robert MacAlpine (later Sir Robert, founder of the famous civil engineering firm) whose nickname was Concrete Bob. It is said that buried within the Glenfinnan Viaduct are a horse and cart that fell headlong into the concrete before it set.

GLENFINNAN Highland Map ref NM9080

Glenfinnan will always have a special place in Scottish history, for it was here that the event which Churchill called 'one of the most audacious and irresponsible enterprises in British history' began – the 1745 Jacobite Rising. The monument tower of 1815, with its 1834 figure of a Highlander, may not be on the spot that Bonnie Prince Charlie unfurled his father's white and red silk banner, yet it is most romantically set at the head of Loch Shiel, overlooking the wooded Eilean Glean Fhianin and the mountains of Sunart and Moidart. Climb the tower for the best views.

The clan chiefs were dismayed that the Prince had brought only seven followers, not the French troops they had expected. They were persuaded to join him only by the example of Cameron of Lochiel, who brought 700 men to Glenfinnan for the Prince. So on 19 August 1745 the banner was set flying, the Old Pretender was proclaimed King James III & VIII, with the Prince as his Regent, and the army – still only 1,200 strong – began its campaign. Taking Edinburgh easily and defeating General Cope in the 15-minute battle at Prestonpans on 21st September, they set out for London. But with little English support and no hope of French help, they turned back at Derby in December and met their doom at Culloden the following April. The story is vividly told in the Visitor Centre nearby, which also traces the Prince's journeys through the Western Highlands and Islands after Culloden.

INVERNESS Highland Map ref NH6616

Inverness is the 'Capital of the Highlands' and a popular holiday centre, set on the banks of the River Ness at the north-eastern extremity of the Great Glen. Commanding the east–west corridor to Moray and Aberdeen as well as the main north–south route through Scotland, its location has given the town a strategic importance that has resulted in a chequered history. The town was probably well established by the time of St Columba's visit in 565AD. Certainly King Duncan (c1010–1040), of Shakespeare's *Macbeth*, had his castle in the town, and various clan chiefs and disaffected Jacobites have stormed through the town over the centuries.

Today Inverness is a busy administrative centre for the Highlands and Islands and presents a mostly 19th-century face. Even the dominating red sandstone walls of Inverness Castle were rebuilt during Victoria's reign as a Sheriff Court and jail, with a monument to Flora Macdonald on the castle esplanade. On the opposite side of the river loom the two massive towers of St Andrew's Episcopal Cathedral, which contains an interesting collection of Russian icons. The Inverness Museum and Art Gallery has fine examples of Highlands artefacts and displays on the archaeology, social and natural history of the Highlands, together with various exhibitions, performances and talks.

From the museum you can see the location of Craig Phadrig, a vitrified fort on a wooded hill west of the River Ness, reached by a steep forest trail. In Huntly Street next to the river you can try out Highland musical instruments at Balnain House or visit the largest kilt-making workshop in Scotland – The Scottish Kiltmaker.

A HIGHLAND WINERY

Few visitors to Scotland would expect to be able to buy locally produced wines, but that is exactly what you can do at Moniack Castle, seven miles (11.3 km) west of Inverness, near Kirkhill. But even the south-facing slopes of the Highland hills cannot support grape-vines, and it is traditional 'country wines' that you will find here – elderflower, silver birch, mead and the delicious sloe gin. This unique Highland enterprise is housed in the former fortress of the Lovat chiefs, where visitors can sample the produce in a wine bar and bistro.

A brilliant display below the castle walls at Inverness

The Ness Islands and the Caledonian Canal

Starting in the historic town of Inverness, this walk quickly takes you out into the rural setting of the midstream islands on the River Ness and along the Caledonian Canal. Easy underfoot, on recognised paths and pavements.

Time: 3 hours (includes exploring one sight of interest).
Distance: 4 miles (6.4 km).
Location: Inverness.
Start: Park in the car park next to St Andrew's Cathedral.
(OS grid ref: NH664448.)
OS Maps: Landranger 26 (Inverness & Strathglass area)
1: 50,000.
Pathfinder 177 (Inverness & Culloden Muir)
Sheet NH 64/74 1: 25,000.
See Key to Walks on page 121.

ROUTE DIRECTIONS

From the car park walk to the bank of the River Ness, turn left and head downstream towards the bridge. Cross over the river, towards **Inverness Castle**, to the **Town House** with its Mercat Cross. Turn immediately right into Castle Street, passing the statue of Flora Macdonald, and take the right-hand fork down View Place to Ness Bank Church and the river. Turn left on the tree-lined bank to the old Iron Bridge and the memorial to the Great War.

From this point you can see the River Ness and its islands. The river flows from Loch Ness, the largest volume of fresh water in the British Isles. After about 55 yards (50 metres) cross the footbridge over the river to the first island, walk over the next white bridge, looking back to view **St Andrew's Cathedral** with its distinctive twin towers. Turn left along the wooded path with pine and beech trees, until you see another unusual curved bridge which crosses from one island to another. Listen to the small rapids, the thunder of water rushing around the islands, and the many waterfowl which are prevalent here. Keep to the left-hand path as it encircles the island to the footbridge.

Cross the bridge to the west bank of the Ness. Turn left and follow the riverbank past 'The Generals Well' until you see the sign, 'Whin Park – No Dogs Allowed'. Turn left, cross the wooden bridge and pass the miniature railway and picnic area. When the path turns to gravel veer to the left, pass the children's play area and walk around the lake, branching to the left at the end before turning right over the wooden bridge into a large field. Keep left next to the river and continue.

At the bottom, near the weir, climb up a series of wooden steps to the **Caledonian Canal**. Turn right at the top with the canal on your left, pass the rowing club and Jacobite Cruises departure point and continue until you come to Bught Road. Turn right, looping back behind the small stone wall, and pass the Bught Floral Hall on the right and Sports Centre on the left. At the Eagle sculpture on the small roundabout turn left along the line of trees in the field and continue until you reach the River Ness. Turn left and walk downstream along the riverbank and make your way back to the car park at St Andrew's Cathedral.

POINTS OF INTEREST

Inverness Castle
Inverness was created a Royal Burgh in 1105 and, during the Scottish War of Independence in the 13th century, the castle was occupied three times by the English, until Robert the Bruce recaptured and destroyed it in 1307. Mary,

Queen of Scots, who was refused entry to a later castle in 1562, had the governor hung from the ramparts. Today's mainly 19th-century sandstone building houses the Sheriffs Court.

The Town House
Built in 1878 in Gothic style, The Town House was once the business heart of the city where merchants plied their wares and public proclamations were made. Previously known as The Exchange, today it is home to the Council Offices. In 1921 this was the venue for the first cabinet meeting to be held outside London; the Prime Minister was David Lloyd George.

St Andrew's Cathedral
The rose-coloured, twin-towered Episcopal Gothic Cathedral was built between 1869–1874 to a design of

Inverness Castle stands proudly above the river

Alexander Ross. Its many features include eleven bells, an unusual octagonal chapterhouse, excellent woodwork in the choir rood screens and stalls, and superb stained glass by John Hardman of Birmingham. The most remarkable artefacts are five golden engraved icons, presented to Bishop Eden, the founder of the cathedral, by the Tsar of Russia in 1861.

Caledonian Canal
Along with the arrival of the railway, Telford's construction of the Caledonian Canal (1802–22) was responsible for the 19th-century development of Inverness. The canal links the lochs of the Great Glen – Loch Lochy, Loch Oich and Loch Ness.

CALEDONIAN PINE FOREST

The Rothiemurchus Estate is one of the few remaining naturally regenerating Caledonian Pine Forests, a precious survivor from the time when much of Scotland was clothed in native pines. Land clearance began in medieval times, when grazing was needed for sheep, and accelerated over the last two centuries or so until the very existence of natural forest areas was under serious threat. Fortunately the threat was recognised just in time, and what was left of the old Caledonian Forest has been actively preserved, offering a haven for the rare crested tit. No forest can be allowed to stand still, though, because survival also depends upon proper management. Rothiemurchus has been worked for centuries and its success can be traced at the Estate Visitor Centre. Guided walks can be booked here.

The Strathspey Steam Railway reopened for business in 1978

KINGUSSIE Highland Map ref NH7500

The little town of Kingussie lies in the beautiful Spey Valley and is home to the Highland Folk Museum, a fascinating place with both indoor and outdoor exhibits. The main house contains traditional furniture and bygones, and a representation of a Highland kitchen; outside you will find a reconstructed Hebridean mill, a salmon smokehouse and a primitive black house from Lewis. There are regular craft demonstrations during the summer months.

Half a mile (0.8 km) south east of the town are the impressive Ruthven Barracks, built in 1718 to help subdue the Highlands. Despite being set on fire by the fleeing Jacobite army, there are considerable remains. The adjacent Insch Marshes Reserve (RSPB) has bird hides and nature trails. You can walk from here to beautiful Glen Tromie (see Walk on page 48).

To the south west a little stream rises, flows east and then northwards picking up tributaries along the way. This is the famous River Spey, one of the foremost salmon rivers in Scotland. The broad Spey Valley is equally renowned for the quality of the malt whisky produced hereabouts – you'll not travel far without spotting the distinctive pointed chimney-caps of a distillery, for there are more than 30 along the river and its tributaries. Pick up the official Malt Whisky Trail for a tour of some of Scotland's finest.

Further north, at Aviemore, the dramatic mountain scenery can be viewed from the comfort of the Strathspey Steam Railway, which runs for five miles (8 km) to Boat of Garten. Aviemore is also well known as a winter sports centre, purpose built to have the appearance of an alpine resort dropped into the Highlands. Incongruous it may be, but Aviemore does provide plenty to do, even when the climate fails to clothe the surrounding slopes with snow, and all year round it is a thriving centre, with shops, conference centres and hotels.

LOCH NESS Highland

It would be difficult for anyone but the most hardened sceptic to gaze out over the waters of Loch Ness without just the small hope of seeing something which might be interpreted as a 'sighting'. Mentioned as long ago as the 7th century, when St Adamnan's *Life of St Columba* tells of the saint calming the creature down after an apparent attack on a monk, the Loch Ness Monster – or, familiarly, Nessie – has become the focus of the tourist industry here. There is a Loch Ness Lodge Visitor Centre with a large-screen cinema, exhibition and sonar scanning cruises; the Official Loch Ness Monster Exhibition in Drumnadrochit has audio-visuals and a 'life-size' model of Nessie; the Original Loch Ness Visitor Centre offers films and boat trips. You can hire a cabin cruiser, or visit ruined Urquhart Castle on the shores of the loch, from where most sightings have been made.

Monster or no, Loch Ness is beautiful and it contains more water than all the lakes and reservoirs in England and Wales put together. It is 24 miles (38.6 km) long, one mile (1.6 km) wide and 750 feet (228.6 metres) deep, making it the largest body of fresh water in Europe. The loch forms a major part of the Caledonian Canal, which links the west coast with the Moray Firth, and follows the line of the Great Glen, cutting Scotland in two. This spectacular geological fault has provided a way through the mountains for centuries of travellers and is followed today by the A82 between Fort William and Inverness.

Urquhart Castle is a popular place for Nessie-spotting

THE CALEDONIAN CANAL
One of the greatest feats of 19th-century engineering, the Caledonian Canal was constructed along the Great Glen by Thomas Telford, who took advantage of the lochs – Lochy, Oich and Ness – which account for about two-thirds of the route. The linking sections of canal have a total of 28 locks, including the famous 'Neptune's Staircase', a series of eight locks at Banavie outside Fort William. Opened in 1822, the canal was originally constructed to provide a safe route for maritime traffic, which had previously had to brave the hazardous seas around the north of Scotland, but the scenic route was soon appreciated by tourists too. By 1900 they were filling three steamboats a day, bound from Inverness to Fort Augustus, Fort William and Oban. Many cruise ships still operate on the canal.

Ruthven Barracks and Insch Marshes

A superb walk across heather-covered moors to a secluded wooded glen and the Insch Marshes Reserve. There are a few high stiles over deer fences, and binoculars are an advantage. The moorland is used by red deer in winter and there is occasional grouse shooting in September, but this should not create any access difficulties.

Time: 4 hours. Distance: 7 miles (11.3 km).
Location: On the B970 half a mile (0.8 km) south of Kingussie.
Start: In the car park opposite Ruthven Barracks.
(OS grid ref: NN764996.)
OS Maps: Landranger 35 (Kingussie & Monadhliath Mountains) 1:50,000.
Pathfinder 253 (Newtownmore) Sheet NN 69/79 1:25,000.
See Key to Walks on page 121.

ROUTE DIRECTIONS

After visiting the remains of **Ruthven Barracks** walk back to the end of the car park, up the bank to a small farm gate and on to a double farm track. Go through a second gate and up through the fields, looking out for views back down to Ruthven, Kingussie, the Spey and Insch Marshes. Keep with the path, looking down to the Burn of Ruthven on your left. On the grassy single track, turn left through the gap in the drystone wall, just before the ruined house. Cross the A-frame ladder over the deer fence, and head down to, and across, the burn.

Take the wide grassy path ahead sweeping uphill past distant television masts on Beinn Bhuidhe. Heather and grouse butts (dug-outs used by grouse-shooters) can be seen on your left. The path veers to the right uphill on to a heather-covered grouse moor. Keep to the well-marked pathway, noticing how the moorland is burnt in patches, to stimulate new growth of heather for the grouse. Near the top veer left leaving the main path for a narrow flat track leading up to a fence on the horizon with a simple gate. Pass through on to a beautiful broad heather moor with cairns. Eventually the path drops downhill past more cairns to a deer fence with a high stile.

Climb the ladder and head downhill into Glentromie with its mature birch woodland and the magnificent River Tromie. Many species of birds can be seen here. Descend into Glentromie and follow waymarkers, keeping to the left, well away from Glen Tromie Lodge, and over the fence until you meet the path along the west bank of the River Tromie. This path eventually emerges beside Torcroy on the B970. From here turn left, and head back along the B970 to Ruthven Barracks, looking out for the RSPB signpost for the **Insch Marshes Reserve**, with its nature trails and bird hides.

POINTS OF INTEREST

Ruthven Barracks
On a mound overlooking the River Spey, these impressive remains date from 1718 and were built after the 1715 rebellion, ostensibly to restore law and order to the region. They replaced a 14th-century castle, and housed Hanoverian forces during the Jacobite rising, but in 1746 they fell to the Stuarts, who set them on fire before making their retreat. The roofless main blocks, parade ground, guard houses and stable are always open.

Red Grouse
Most grouse moors came into existence between 1800 and 1840, reaching their peak in the 1860s, with the introduction of the breach-loading gun. Until recently grouse moors covered three million acres of Scotland. Grouse are the most widespread game birds in the British Isles, and although population numbers fluctuate periodically, the recent declining numbers are currently causing concern. Their popularity as a game bird stems from their extremely fast flight when driven by beaters over carefully situated gun butts. The Highlands are their native stronghold, and populations increase with good moor management, through rotational patchwork burning, ensuring continuous new growth of ling heather shoots, their staple diet.

Insch Marshes Reserve

The freshwater marshes in Upper Strathspey are important for breeding waders and wintering waterfowl. Flocks of whooper swans from Iceland overwinter here between late September and April, and a variety of waterfowl, including mallard, teal, widgeon and tufted duck are resident in the winter months. There is also a population of roe deer who come to feed here.

The intimidating walls of Ruthven Barracks still stand

WEST HIGHLAND LINE
Mallaig is the terminus of the West Highland Line, which is celebrated as one of Britain's most scenic railway routes. Its construction was no easy task – the peat bogs of Rannoch Moor were traversed with a floating bed of brushwood, beneath tonnes of ash and earth; the rocky heights of Glenfinnan and the deeply indented coastline had to be crossed. Contractor Robert MacAlpine pioneered the structural use of concrete, building the high viaducts which give such magnificent views. Sit on the left for the outward journey (reserve a seat at peak times).

The lonely little church by the road to Mallaig has provided a location for several films

MALLAIG   Highland Map ref NM6796

This small, busy fishing harbour, facing the Isle of Skye across the Sound of Sleat, stands at the end of the A830 from Fort William, more romantically known as the 'Road to the Isles'. The term comes from the cattle-droving days, before the railway arrived in 1901, but it holds the evocative promise of a special destination for today's travellers. It is also the last stop on the famous West Highland Line, and ferries from Mallaig can take you on to Skye, Rum, Eigg, Muck and Canna.

A couple of miles away at Morar the waters of Scotland's deepest freshwater loch tumble down a spectacular waterfall and into a beautiful sandy bay. One of the lovely beaches along here provided the setting for the film *Local Hero*, and the drive southwards is enchanting, passing through woodland of beech, oak and birch, with fine views out to the islands. Give yourself plenty of time here – it's a slow, winding road and largely single track until you reach the little church above Lochailort.

This part of the west coast has many associations with Prince Charles Edward Stuart. It was at Loch Nan Uamh, south of Arisaig, that the Prince landed in 1745 to raise an army, and it was from here that he left for France after defeat at Culloden the following year, leaving in his wake a tide of government retribution against the Highlanders.

Inverness

Leisure Information

Places of Interest

Shopping

The Performing Arts

Sports, Activities

and the Outdoors

Annual Events and Customs

Checklist

Leisure Information

TOURIST INFORMATION CENTRES

Aviemore
Grampian Road. Tel: 01479 810363.
Carrbridge
Main Street (seasonal). Tel: 01479 841630.
Daviot Wood
A9, by Inverness (seasonal). Tel: 01463 772203.
Fort Augustus
Car Park (seasonal). Tel: 01320 366367.
Fort William
Cameron Square. Tel: 01397 70 3781.
Grantown-on-Spey
High Street (seasonal) Tel: 01479 872773.
Inverness
Castle Wynd. Tel: 01463 234353.
Kingussie
King Street (seasonal). Tel: 01540 661297.
Kyle of Lochalsh
Car Park (seasonal). Tel: 01599 4276.
Mallaig
(Seasonal.) Tel: 01687 2170.
Ralia
A9, north by Newtonmore (seasonal). Tel: 01540 673253.
Spean Bridge
(Seasonal.) Tel: 01397 712576.

OTHER INFORMATION

Ferries
Caledonian MacBrayne Ferries, Ferry Terminal, Gourock. Tel: 01475 650100. For Hebrides via Firth of Clyde and west-coast ports; sailings to 23 islands. 'Rover' tickets available.
Forest Enterprise
Forestry Commision, 231 Corstorphine Road, Edinburgh. Tel: 0131 334 0303.
Historic Scotland
Longmore House, Salisbury Place, Edinburgh. Tel: 0131 668 8800.
National Trust for Scotland
5 Charlotte Square, Edinburgh. Tel: 0131 226 5922.
Royal Society for the Protection of Birds
17 Regent Terrace, Edinburgh. Tel: 0131 556 5624.
Scottish Tourist Board
23 Ravelston Terrace, Edinburgh. Tel: 0131 332 2433.
Scottish Wildlife Trust
16 Cramond Glebe Road, Edinburgh. Tel: 0131 312 7765.
Weather
Great Outdoors Weatherline. Tel: 0891 567538. Mountaincall for north-west Scotland. Tel: 0891 505680. Western Highlands, Climbing line. Tel: 0891 200819. Weathercall for north-west Scotland. Tel: 0891 500425.

ORDNANCE SURVEY MAPS

Landranger 1:50,000 sheet numbers 25, 26, 33, 34, 35, 36, 40, 41, 42, 43, 49, 50, 51. Outdoor Leisure 1:25,000 sheet number 8.

Places of Interest:

There will be an admission charge at the following places of interest unless otherwise stated.
Balnain House
40 Huntly Street, Inverness. Tel: 01463 713611. Open: all year, most days.
Clan MacPherson House and Museum
Newtonmore. Tel: 01540 673332. Open: May–Sep most days. Free.
Clava Cairns
Off B9006, 8½ miles (13.7 km) east of Inverness. Tel: 0131 668 8800. Always open. Free.
Corrimony Cairn
Glen Urquhart. 8½ miles (13.7 km) west of Drumnadrochit. Tel: 0131 668 8800. Always open.
Culloden Battlefield
Culloden Moor. B9006, 5 miles (8 km) east of Inverness. Tel: 01463 790607. Open: site all year daily; visitor centre early Feb-late Dec daily.
Dochfour Gardens
A82, 6 miles (9.7 km) south west of Inverness. Tel: 01463 861254.

Open: Apr–Oct most days.

Eilean Donan Castle
Off the A87 at Dornie. Tel: 01599 555202. Open: Easter–Sep daily.

Fort Augustus Abbey and Fort
Tel: 01320 366232. Open: May–Sep most days.

Glencoe and North Lorn Folk Museum
Glencoe village. Open: mid May–Sep, most days.

Glencoe Visitor Centre
Glencoe. Tel: 01855 811307. Open: Apr–late Oct.

Glenelg Brochs
Twelve miles (19.3 km) west of Shiel Bridge. Tel: 0131 668 8800. Always open. Free.

Highland Folk Museum
Kingussie. Tel: 01540 661307. Open: all year most days.

Illegal Moidart Museum
Mingarry. Tel: 01967 431662. Open: Apr–Sep most days.

Inverness Museum and Art Gallery
Castle Wynd, Inverness. Tel: 01463 237114. Open: all year most days. Free.

Landmark Highland Heritage and Adventure Park
Carrbridge. Tel: 01479 841613. Open: all year daily.

Lochalsh Woodland Garden
Off A87, 3 miles (4.8 km) east of Kyle of Lochalsh. Tel: 01599 566207. Open: May–late Sep most days

Loch an Eilein Visitor Centre
Rothiemurchus Estate, On B970 2½ miles (4 km) south of Aviemore. Tel: 01479 810858. Open: all year most days.

Mallaig Marine World
The Harbour, Mallaig. Tel: 01687 462292. Open: all year daily.

Official Loch Ness Monster Exhibition
Drumnadrochit. Tel: 01456 450573/450218. Open: all year daily.

Original Loch Ness Visitor Centre
Drumnadrochit. Tel: 01456 450342. Open: all year daily.

Ruthven Barracks
Kingussie. Tel: 0131 668 8800. Always open. Free.

The Scottish Kiltmaker
Huntly Street, Inverness. Tel: 01463 222781. Open: all year most days.

Strathspey Steam Railway
Aviemore–Boat of Garten). Tel: 01479 810725. Open: Jun–Sep most days; certain days Apr, May, Oct, Dec and Jan.

Treasures of the Earth
Mallaig Road, Corpach. Tel: 01397 772283. Open: Feb–Dec daily.

Urquhart Castle
near Drumnadrochit. Tel: 0131 668 8800. Open: all year most days.

West Highland Museum
Cameron Square, Fort William. Tel: 01397 702169. Open: all year most days.

SPECIAL INTEREST FOR CHILDREN

The following places may be of interest to visitors with children. Unless otherwise stated there will be an admission charge.

Cairngorm Reindeer Centre
Glen More, Aviemore (A951). Tel: 01479 861228. Open: all year daily.

Craig Highland Farm
Two miles (3.2 km) east of Plockton on shore road to Stromeferry. Tel: 01599 544205.

Highland Wildlife Park
Kincraig. Tel: 01540 651270. Open: Apr–Oct daily.

The Performing Arts

Eden Court Theatre
Bishop's Road, Inverness. Tel: 01463 239861.

Shopping

LOCAL SPECIALITIES

Cloth
James Pringle Weavers of Inverness. Holm Woollen Mills, Dores Road, Inverness. Tel: 01463 223490 for details.

Country wines
Highland Wineries, Moniack Castle, Kirkhill. Tel: 01463 831283.

Distilleries
Ben Nevis Distillery, Fort William. Tel: 01397 700200. Open: all year most days.

Dalwhinnie Distillery, off A9 on road to Perth. Tel: 01528 522208. Open: all year most days. Tomatin Distillery, 6 miles (9.7 km) south east of Inverness off the A9. Tel: 01808 511234. Open: Mar–Oct, most days.

Mineral water
Lovat Mineral Water. Off A831 Fanellan, just south of Beauly. Tel: 01463 74620.

Pottery
Loch an Eilein Pottery, south west of Aviemore on B970. Tel: 01479 810837.

Sports, Activities and the Outdoors

ANGLING

There are ample opportunities for angling of all kinds in the area. Enquire at local Tourist Information Offices.

BOAT TRIPS

Inverness, Loch Ness and Caledonian Canal
British Waterways, Inverness. Tel: 01463 233140. Caledonian Canal, Seaport Marina, Inverness. Tel: 01463 233140 (canal), or 01463 239745 (marina). Jacobite Cruises. Tel: 01463 233999. On A82, 1¼ miles (2 km) from Inverness; courtesy bus from Tourist Information Centre. Loch Ness Yacht Charters, Dochgarroch, Inverness. Tel: 01463 861303. Caley Cruises, Canal Road, Inverness. Tel: 01463 236328.

CHAIR LIFTS

Cairngorm Chair Lift
Aviemore. Tel: 01479 861261. Open: all year daily, weather permitting.

Glencoe Chair Lift (White Corries)
Off A82 by Kingshouse. Tel: 01855 851226. Open: Jan–Apr, most days; Jun–Sep daily.

CLAY-PIGEON SHOOTING

Rothiemurchus Estate Visitor Centre
One mile (1.6 km) from Aviemore. Tel: 01479 810858. Open: all year daily.

COUNTRY PARKS, FORESTS AND NATURE RESERVES

Insh Marshes Reserve
Adjacent to Ruthven Barracks, Kingussie.

Glen Affric
South west of Cannich off A831. Contact Forest Enterprise, Strathoich, Fort Augustus.

Loch Garten Nature Reserve
Eight miles (12.9 km) north east of Aviemore off the B970. Tel: 01479 831694 /831476.

Reelig Glen
Moniack. A862, 8 miles (12.9 km) west of Inverness.

CYCLING

The Great Glen Cycle Route
Off the A82 Fort William–Inverness road, through forests on gravel surface. Contact Fort Augustus Forest Enterprise Tel: 01320 366322.

CYCLE HIRE

Arisaig
Bespoke Highland Cycle Tours, The Bothy, Camusdarach. Tel: 01687 450272/0141 334 9017.

Aviemore
Pine Bank Chalets, Dalfaber Road. Tel: 01479 810000.

Fort William
Lee's Cycle Hire. Leesholme, Cameron Road. Tel: 01397 704204. Nevis Range, Torlundy, Fort William. Tel: 01397 705825.

Grantown-on-Spey
Logans Bike Hire. 'Crann-Tara' Guesthouse, High Street. Tel: 01479 872197.

Great Glen Cycle Route
Great Glen School of Adventure, South Laggan, Spean Bridge. Tel: 01809 501381.

Inverness
Thornton Cycles, 23 Castle Street. Tel: 01463 222810.

Spean Bridge
Nevis Cycles. Tel: 01397 712404.
Strathspey Adventure. 'Ryoan', Carrbridge. Tel: 01479 841667.

DRY SKI SLOPE

Kincraig
Loch Insch Watersports and Boathouse Restaurant, between Kingussie and Aviemore. Tel: 01540 651272.

GOLF COURSES

Boat of Garten
Boat of Garten Golf Club. Tel: 01479 831282.

Carrbridge
Carrbridge Golf Club. Tel: 01479 841623.

Fort William
Fort William Golf Club. Tel: 01397 704464.

Grantown-on-Spey
Grantown-on-Spey Golf Club. Tel: 01479 872079.

Inverness
Inverness Golf Club, Culcabock. Tel: 01463 239882.

Kingussie
Kingussie Golf Club, Gynack Road. Tel: 01540 661374.

Newtonmore
Newtonmore Golf Club, Golf Course Road. Tel: 01540 673328.

GUIDED WALKS

Five Sisters of Kintail
Visitor centre at Morvich. Tel: 01599 511219 for information.

Rothiemurchus Estate
A mile (1.6 km) from Aviemore. Tel: 01479 810858.

HORSE-RIDING

Aviemore
Alvie Stables. Tel: 01540 651409.

Carrbridge
Carrbridge Trekking Centre, Ellan Bridge Stables, Station Road. Tel: 01479 841602.

Drumnadrochit
Highland Riding Centre. Tel: 01456 450220.

Fort Augustus
Fort Augustus Riding Centre. Tel: 01320 366418.

Grantown-on-Spey
The Strathspey Highland Pony Centre. Tel: 01479 873073.

Kingussie
Ballintean Riding Centre. Kincraig. Tel: 01540 651352.

Newtonmore
Croila Trekking Centre, Golf Course Road. Tel: 01540 673742.

SAILING

Inverness
Highland Drascombe Sailing School, North Kessock. Tel: 01463 731493.

Loch Insh
Watersports, Kincraig. Tel: 01540 651272

Loch Morlich
Watersports, by Aviemore Tel: 01479 861221.

Fort William
Snowgoose Activities, Corpach. Tel: 01397 772467.

SKIING

Aviemore Mountain Resort
Tel: 01479 810624.

Glencoe (White Corries)
Tel: 01855 811303.

Cairngorm by Aviemore
Tel: 01479 861261.

Nevis Range
Torlundy. Off A82, signposted 'Aonach Mor'. Tel: 01397 705825.

WATERSPORTS

Abernethy Outdoor Centre, Nethybridge. Tel: 01479 821279. Great Glen School of Adventure, South Laggan by Spean Bridge (water skiing). Tel: 01809 501223. Loch Insch Watersports, between Kingussie and Aviemore. (Canoeing, sailing, windsurfing). Tel: 01540 651272. Loch Morlich Watersports, by Aviemore Tel: 01479 861221. Snowgoose Activities, Corpach, Fort William. Tel: 01397 772467

Annual Events and Customs

Aviemore
Sled-dog rally, late January. Rothiemurchus International Highland Games, late July.

Drumnadrochit
Glenurquhart Highland Gathering and Games, late August.

Grantown-on-Spey
Torchlight Procession, late December.

Inverness
Folk Festival, Easter weekend. Inverness Highland Games, late July.
Inverness Tattoo, late July.

Kingussie
Badenoch & Strathspey Music Festival, late March.
Shinty (Camanachd Cup Final), First Saturday in June.

The Hebrides
INNER HEBRIDES

This group of islands which lies off the ragged west coast of Scotland is steeped in the history and legends of the land. Skye is the largest and most northerly of the group – and the most accessible since the opening of the road bridge from Kyle of Lochalsh. It is also very picturesque, with the beautiful Cuillins rising up in the south before dropping to a coastline of deep indentations and rocky headlands. But each of the islands has its own distinctive charm: Coll and Tiree are low-lying and fertile; Rum is a National Nature Reserve; Eigg has its 'singing sands' and much geological interest; Muck is far more pleasant than its name might suggest.

BURROWING BIRDS
The elusive Manx shearwater, *Puffinus puffinus*, which comes in to land only under cover of darkness, has been breeding in burrows on Rum for centuries. The Vikings, alarmed at hearing their strange calls from underground, named the westernmost mountain Trollival, or 'the place of the trolls'.

COLL AND TIREE

Like Harris and Lewis, the low island of Coll is made up of Lewisian gneiss, the oldest rock in Europe, exposures of which can be seen in the rocky approach to the harbour at Arinagour. Inland, peat bogs dotted with lochans give way in the west to silvery beaches, with sand dunes reaching to a height of over 100 feet (30.5 metres). The crofting community here was once 2,000 strong, and rich pastureland led to production of the island's own special cheese. Today, visitors come to enjoy the peace and tranquillity, or to fish for brown trout in the lochans. There are many reminders of more ancient inhabitants, with the standing stones at Totronald, a cairn at Arinagour and a number of Iron-Age forts to explore – have a look at Dun an Achaidh and Feall Bay. In the south of the island, Breacacha Castle dates from around 1450 and was built by the

Breacacha Castle looms on the shoreline to the south of Coll

Macleans, one-time lairds of Coll.

Tiree's Gaelic name meant 'land of corn', and it is certainly very fertile. The island is low-lying and somewhat windswept, but this does not detract from its appeal to visitors – indeed, it is a positive attraction to those who come for the surfing, and is more than made up for by a record rate of sunshine. There are prehistoric remains to explore, including the broch of Dun Mor Vaul, and between Vaul and Balephetrish lies the 'ringing stone' which is covered with over 50 Bronze-Age cup marks.

These two neighbouring islands, north west of Mull, can be reached by ferry from Oban, and Tiree has connecting flights from Glasgow and Barra.

RUM, EIGG, MUCK AND CANNA

Rum's four high pinnacles make it the most easily recognised of the Small Isles – the tallest peak, Askival, reaches 2,592 feet (810 metres) – and there are semi-precious stones in the rocks of these mountains. The only settlement is at the head of Loch Scresort, where the wonderfully eccentric Victorian Kinloch House, now a hotel, is a reminder of the days when the island was a private sportsman's paradise overrun with specially introduced red deer. It is a strangely desolate island, its crofters cleared long ago. In 1957 the Nature Conservancy Council (now Scottish Natural Heritage) purchased Rum. Today the island is managed as a national nature reserve and biosphere reserve, and gradually the native vegetation and wildlife, including white-tailed sea eagles, are being restored. Two nature

The circular walls of Tiree's Dun Mor Vaul can still be clearly identified

SAILOR BEWARE!
Scores of sailing boats take to the waters around the west coast of Scotland, which are a delightful, if challenging, playground. The Western Isles offer several distinctive hazards to sailors, quite apart from the expected rigours of weather and submerged rocks. If you are relying on your compass to find your way past Canna, then watch out, because Compass Hill, just to the north of the harbour, is particularly rich in iron deposits and is said to interfere with navigational compasses. And if you thought of taking a short cut between the islands of Jura and Scarba, think again – the Corrievreckan whirlpool could break you up in no time.

TEMPERANCE REJECTED
George Bullough, the son of a Lancastrian industrialist and builder of Kinloch House, renamed his private paradise island Rhum, to distinguish it from the devilish drink, and perhaps to suggest something more whimsical and exotic. However, in 1992 the Nature Conservancy Council, aware that there is no 'rh' prefix in the Gaelic, changed it firmly back again.

trails can be followed through the woodland from Kinloch House.

Washed in ever-changing light, Eigg has been likened to an upturned boat, its prow formed by the sweeping cliffs of the Sgurr (1289ft/393m), a dramatic pitchstone ridge to the south of the island. The sheltering rock wall has created a sub-tropical micro-climate on the island. The island flora, which includes rare ferns and palm trees, is incredibly rich. In the bay of Laig, to the north west, there are 'singing sands' of quartzite. Two hundred islanders were massacred by marauding MacLeods from Skye as they hid in the cave of Uamh Fhraing on the southern coastline, back in 1577. The story is told in Sir Walter Scott's poem 'The Lord of the Isles'. Eigg was a power base for the MacDonalds of Clanranald, but when the family fell on hard times in 1828 the island was sold, and a succession of owners have attempted to stabilise the crofting community here.

Muck, a mere two miles (3.2km) by one mile (1.6km), is the smallest, lowest and most isolated of the Small Isles. Gently sloping and comparatively fertile, Muck supports a small community which is successfully run as a model island unit by its paternalistic laird, from Gallanach House.

Canna is the most westerly and perhaps the most attractive of this island group, its northern cliffs noisy with seabirds. Spring arrives early here, and the land is comparatively rich and fertile. There are remains of an early nunnery on the island. Like Eigg, Canna was sold by the MacDonalds of Clanranald in the early years of the 19th century, and later attracted a succession of benevolent owners. The last of these, the Gaelic scholar John Lorne Campbell, presented it to the National Trust for Scotland in 1981.

The view from Arisaig's sandy shoreline to the steep peaks of Rum, with the cliffs of Eigg to the left

SKYE AND RAASAY

Skye is the largest and most famous of the Inner Hebrides, dominated from every view by the high peaks of the Cuillins. The jagged gabbro of the Black Cuillins and the pink, scree-covered granite of the Red Cuillins have proved an irresistable challenge for mountaineers, and the most inaccessible peaks were only conquered at the end of the last century. To the north on the Trotternish peninsula is an extraordinary broken ridge from which peaks and pillars loom eerily on a misty day.

Road signs in Gaelic as well as English quickly tell you you're in a different culture, and Skye retains a strong Gaelic identity, encouraged at the college, Sabhal Mor Ostaig, in Sleat. At the Aros Heritage Centre, just south of Portree, a forest walk illustrates the letters of the Gaelic alphabet. The centre also offers one of the best introductions to the history of Skye. Through a 45-minute audio tour the story is told of the crofters and their struggles to survive the hardships of the land, famine and poverty after the 1745 rebellion. There are many tales, including one of a chieftain who tried to sell his people into slavery in the Colonies, and of the famous riots on neighbouring Raasay, in 1882. This civil disturbance led directly to the Crofters' Act of 1886, controlling rent and tenure for the first time, which is still in place today. Further crofting museums at Colbost and Luib have reconstructed homesteads.

The Uig ferry will transport you onwards from Skye to North Uist or Lewis

OLD MACDONALD
Duntulm was a Macdonald stronghold famous for its hospitality. However, the story is told of one chief who discovered that his heir planned his murder when an invitation to dinner was mixed up accidentally with the instructions to the hired assassin. The treacherous heir was thrown into the dungeon at Duntulm, with nothing to eat but salt beef, and no water to quench his thirst. The legend continues that in later years a skeleton was discovered still clutching an empty mug.

A FAIRY TOKEN

A threadbare scrap of cloth, faded almost beyond recognition and displayed safely behind glass, is one of Scotland's best-loved talismans. This is the Fairy Flag of the MacLeods, supposedly presented to a clan chief, back in the mists of time, by his fairy lover, who promised that aid would be forthcoming if the cloth were waved in times of dire need. The flag has been used twice to turn the course of battle, apparently with great success, giving the lie to spoil-sports who claim it is a banner stolen from Harold Hardrada in 1066.

Portree is the island's capital, its colour-washed houses round the harbour pleasing on the eye. This little town was named after a royal visit in 1540 by James V – *port righ* means king's harbour – and its formal square is a miniature delight. Portree is the gateway to the Trotternish peninsula; taking the road up the eastern side, look out for the distinctive column of the Old Man of Storr and other strange rock formations up on your left, and for the columnar formations and dramatic waterfall at the Kilt Rock on the coast to your right, just before Staffin – there are marvellous views from here across to the blue hills of the mainland.

Continuing around this long finger of land you pass ruined Duntulm Castle and a memorial to Flora Macdonald, the Jacobite heroine who smuggled Prince Charles Edward Stuart here from his hiding place in South Uist in 1746. The Prince, disguised as 'Betty Burke', continued his escape to Raasay and then on to France. Flora was arrested and briefly imprisoned in the Tower of London. She later married a Skye man and emigrated to America; they returned to live down the coast at Kingsborough, and Flora's grave is there.

Heading west from Portree brings you to the wilder side of the island, with the Waternish and Duinish peninsulas like two long fingers reaching out towards the Outer Hebrides. Dunvegan is the family seat of another powerful Skye clan, the MacLeods, and claims to be Scotland's oldest inhabited castle, occupied since the 13th century. Surrounded by a stout wall, and heavily restored and harled in the mid-19th century, the castle is impressive if not beautiful, but the treasures in its richly furnished rooms are well worth a look.

Heavily restored in Victorian times, Dunvegan Castle is the seat of the MacLeods of Skye

Broadford is the main centre for exploring the south of the island, and with its concentration of craftspeople, it is a good place to seek out good-quality souvenirs. Definitely not a place to get something to take home, but a good place to visit, is the award-winning Reptile Centre, or Serpentarium. Here you can handle snakes and learn a lot more about their way of life.

If the weather is clear, don't miss a drive over to Elgol to experience some of Britain's most magnificent scenery. The road winds below the mighty Red Cuillins and beside Loch Slapin before descending an alarmingly steep road into Elgol (not for caravans). You can see across to the island of Soay, with Canna, Rum and Eigg to the south. Try to make time for a boat trip, which offers a dramatic glimpse of spectacular Loch Coruisk.

After the barrenness of the mountains, Sleat seems a veritable Garden of Eden. Surrounded by lovely woodland gardens, the Clan Donald Centre by Armadale is well worth a visit. There is an excellent museum, exhibitions, genealogical research facilities, guided walks, a restaurant and much more. Look out for special events in summer.

Skye is an unlikely crossroads among the islands. You can reach it by ferry from Mallaig (about 40 minutes), or across the strong currents by Glenelg (summer only), or across the new bridge at Kyle of Lochalsh. The bridge has provoked controversy, particularly over its tolls, but at least it is low enough to be unobtrusive and must be a relief to those who have watched the hours of their holiday tick away as they wait for the little ferry. Ferries to the outer islands leave from the harbour at Uig, on the Trotternish peninsula, and to Raasay from Sconser.

Looking across to Blaven from Torrin, on the winding road to Elgol

OTTERS
Many people hope to spot wild otters around the shores and lochs of Scotland, and, given a bit of luck, a good pair of binoculars and some local guidance, there is every chance you will. The Kylerhea Otter Sanctuary on Skye is a good place to learn more about these shy creatures, and to seek advice on where and when to look. Loch Sunart on the southern coast of the Ardnamurchan peninsula, Loch Spelve in Mull and Loch Eynort in South Uist are all good places to look.

Camasunary Bay and the Black Cuillins

Some of the most spectacular scenery on Skye, with magnificent views of Camasunary Bay, the island of Rum, and the Black Cuillins. A strenuous walk, which may be shortened by omitting the stretch to Loch na Creitheach. Good waterproof footwear is recommended.

Time: 5 hours continuous walking. Distance: 8½ miles (13.7 km), can be shortened to 6 miles (9.7 km).
Location: 15 miles (24 km) west of Broadford.
Start: From Broadford take the B8083 (formerly the A881) signposted 'Elgol'. The road passes through Torrin and along the shore of Loch Slapin. Drive past the sign for Old Kilmarie Graveyard, and park in the layby on the left opposite a farm gate. (OS grid ref: NG545172.)
OS Maps: Landranger 21 (South Skye) 1:50,000.
Outdoor Leisure 8 (The Cuillins & Torridon Hills) 1:25,000.
See Key to Walks on page 121.

ROUTE DIRECTIONS

Cross the road to the farm gate, ignoring the sign 'No footbridge to Camasunary', which is irrelevant to this walk. Step over the stile, and walk uphill, over a burn, and towards the distant trees. As the path levels look down to the right where you will see a small lochan and the nearby remains of a stone circle.

Cross the stepping stones of two burns and follow the path up the steep slope towards Am Mam, passing through a farm gate. Here there are cairns and, over the top of Am Mam on the left, panoramic views of Loch Scavaig and the islands of Soay, **Rum** and Canna. Soon the magnificent sweep of **Camasunary Bay** backed by lush green meadows and the dramatic **Black Cuillin Hills** come into view. The path curves to the right and drops downhill.

Fifty five yards (50 metres) before a hairpin bend, and next to a small cairn on the right, step up on to a peaty path to the right, for the loop along Loch na Creitheach. Alternatively, to shorten the walk, take the hairpin path to the bay and back again.

For Loch na Creitheach continue on the peaty path (boggy in wet weather), following the contours. Cross the pretty River Abhainn nan Leac with its waterfalls, and head for the cleft in the rocks between An t-Sron and Bla Bheinn. Walk alongside the stream and through the gap until the superb view of Loch na Creitheach comes into sight. Descend the heathery slope on the path which now runs almost parallel to the loch; two-thirds of the way down you will see a drystone dyke and the return path along the lochside. At an

appropriate point walk down to the loch through one of the dry gullies, turn left and walk alongside the loch. Head towards the beach of Camasunary Bay along the clear path, passing a ruined house. To the right you can see a huge cross at the base of **Sgurr Hain**. At the house by the beach turn right and walk across the machair to the picturesque white bothy. Return to the house and turn right following the path over the wooden bridge. After the hairpin bend turn right and follow the path uphill to Am Màm and down to Kilmarie.

POINTS OF INTEREST

Rum

One of the most spectacular of the Inner Hebrides, Rum contains the earliest settlements of Mesolithic man to be found in Scotland. The

Camasunary Bay

One of the most beautiful bays in Skye, its Gaelic meaning is 'Bay of the Fair Shieling' (pasture). At the far end of the beach lies a bothy – once a simple dwelling for farm servants, but now a temporary shelter for walkers and climbers.

The Black Cuillins

Described by some as the finest mountain skyline in Scotland, the Black Cuillins include some 20 munros (peaks over 3,000 feet/914.4 metres). The name is popularly believed to be derived from Cu Chulainn, a legendary

Peaceful Camasunary Bay opens out below walkers on the ridge of Am Mam

hunter who crossed from Ireland to Skye in two mighty strides. A favourite haunt of climbers, geologists and walkers, the Cuillins have also captured the imagination of artists and poets, including J M W Turner and Sir Walter Scott.

The Cross at Sgurr Hain

Best seen from the path above Camasunary Bay, the huge cross is on the eastern face of Sgurr Hain, close to its base. It is of unknown provenance or age.

name of the island was reverted from Rhum to the Gaelic spelling Rum in 1991 by the Nature Conservancy Council, who, as owners of the island, are encouraging its natural vegetation and wildlife.

THE OUTER HEBRIDES

Known also as the Western Isles, this chain of islands, which includes Lewis and Harris, North and South Uist, Benbecula and Barra, is linked by a series of causeways and ferry crossings. Almost treeless, the Outer Hebrides are composed of some of the world's oldest rock, which lies beneath a layer of peat carpeted with heather and grass. Here also are some of Britain's most attractive Atlantic beaches, backed by fertile coastal plains known as 'machairs'. Everywhere are reminders of ancient islanders – cairns and tombs, forts and churches.

BARRA

Little Barra is a mere five miles (8 km) wide by eight miles (12.9 km) long. You can reach it by ferry from Lochboisdale or Oban, arriving at the main settlement of Castlebay. The 11th-century castle in the harbour here, Kiessimul, was a stronghold of the MacNeills, a ruffianly clan noted for their piratical raids on the shores of Northern Ireland – a little boat will take you across on open days. Many visitors choose to fly in to Barra, however, landing on the long silvery beach of Traigh Mhor to the north of the island. It's the only beach in Britain that doubles as a runway for commercial flights (tides permitting). There are more splendid sandy beaches on the western side of the island. Gaelic culture thrives here – look out for the Barra Feis, a lively summer festival.

HARRIS AND LEWIS

Harris and Lewis are often assumed to be two islands, but they are one, linked by a narrow neck of land. Harris, to the south, is the gem of the Outer Isles, with an exceptionally beautiful, if subtle, landscape which has been the inspiration as well as a source of materials and

FLORA AND FAUNA

The coastline, freshwater, hills, moors and mountains of the Outer Hebrides provide a wide variety of habitats for over 700 species of flowering plants and ferns. Acid-tolerant plants, such as heathers, grow in peat, while the delicate wild pansy, silverweed and orchids abound on the machair. On the moorland lochs waterlilies are found, while at higher altitudes the alpine lady's mantle thrives.

This is also a birdwatcher's paradise, with more than 300 species recorded, at least 107 of which breed here. Cormorants, greylag geese, shelduck, common eider and whooper swans are often seen, and the elusive corncrake is still to be heard from the long grass. Red- and black-throated divers occur on the more remote moorland lochs. There are occasional sightings of the golden eagle and, on Benbecula, the short-eared owl. In the old woodlands near Lews Castle treecreepers and grey wagtails can be seen.

Castlebay, Barra with Kiessimul Castle in the centre

dyes for the famous Harris weavers – roads are dotted with signs inviting you to the cottage workshops.

The main village is Tarbert (*Tairbeart*), which is also the ferry terminal from Skye. The beaches and clear blue water here are magnificent. In the south, St Clement's Church houses some remarkable carvings; with the tomb of Alexander Macleod, they form the finest group of late medieval sculptures in the Western Isles. Leverburgh, just up the coast, was named after Lord Leverhulme, who purchased the islands in 1918 and did his best to encourage industry here.

The ruins of an old whaling station can be seen at Bunavoneadar. The large brick chimney seems incongruous in this landscape, but it is a reminder of the former importance of the whaling industry.

Lewis has great undulating blanket peat moors, hundreds of lochs and is inhabited by at least 750 weavers. Sabbath observance is taken very seriously here, so most places close on Sundays. The busy fishing port of Stornoway is the only town and the administrative centre. The woodlands of nearby Lews Castle were imported, with their earth, in the 19th century.

The Black House at Arnol is a traditional Hebridean dwelling open as a museum to illustrate the life of a crofting family. Further south along the coast is the ancient tower of Dun Carloway Broch, an Iron-Age dwelling which still stands about 30 feet (9.1 metres) high. South from here is the impressive Callanish site, with a circle of 13 standing stones and an avenue of 19 monoliths, probably from between 3000 and 1500BC. Revealed from the peat in the 19th century, Callanish is considered second only to Stonehenge in importance.

The Standing Stones of Callanish may once have been used for sun worship

HARRIS TWEED
This famous cloth is made on treadle looms only on the island with two names – Lewis and Harris. It was Lady Dunmore, the wife of the Laird of the Islands, who introduced the cloth to the British aristocracy in the 1840s, thus providing the islanders with a way of making an income from their own skills. The Harris Tweed Authority states that 'Harris tweed must be made from 100 per cent pure virgin wool, dyed, spun and finished in the Outer Hebrides and hand woven by the islanders in their own homes.' Now fashion designers from Europe to Japan and the United States use the cloth, which is traditionally associated with sporting clothes. Always check for the famous Orb mark, the proof that a piece of cloth is authentic.

Neatly hung stones secure the roof of this croft house at Carinish, on North Uist

CORNCRAKES
It is rare on mainland Britain to hear the distinctive 'crek crek' sound of the corncrake, although this grassland bird was once much more widespread. Corncrakes need tall vegetation such as rough grass and iris beds between April and June to provide safe cover. Unfortunately their preferred hay field habitats on the mainland have been largely destroyed by intensive mechanised agriculture, which is thankfully not practised in the crofts of the Hebrides. These islands now hold most of the small relict British breeding population of these migratory birds, which spend their winters in Asia and Africa. See or hear them on the RSPB's Balranald Reserve.

NORTH UIST AND BENBECULA

The island of North Uist lies amid a scattering of smaller islands, with abundant lochans and magnificent white sandy beaches (especially around the north). Fertile lush green machair in the west rises to low mountains on the eastern side.

The main village and ferry terminal for the Cal-Mac Ferry from Tarbert (Harris) and Uig (Skye) is Lochmaddy. From here you can explore the RSPB's Balranald Nature Reserve, at Hougharry (*Hogha Gearraidh*), with its small croft-house converted into an informative visitor centre. Originally created for the protection of the red-necked phalarope, the reserve is well worth a visit.

North of Sollas lies Udal, a village which was completely covered by sand in 1697, but which shows evidence of continual habitation for about 4,000 years, from the Bronze Age right through to the 19th century. North Uist has a notable concentration of chambered cairns, and the best of these, at Barpa Langass, can be seen from the roadside. The splendid ruin of Trinity Temple (*Teampull na Trionaid*), a medieval monastery near Carinish, is a former centre of learning for the sons of chiefs.

Benbecula, often described as a stepping stone between the Uists, has a causeway that spans the mesmerising mosaic of freshwater lochs, sea lochs, and sandbanks. This is an excellent place for birdwatching, a little fishing or simply relaxing in beautiful surroundings. There is a cave in the only prominent hill, Rueval, which is where Prince Charles Edward Stuart hid in 1746. It was from here, dressed as Betty Burke, that he travelled east to Rossinish Point and made his famous crossing to Skye and freedom, assisted by Flora Macdonald. The army base at Balivanich is a centre of activity on the island, and continues a long history of military activity beginning well before the Iron Age at Dun Gainhich (*Dunganachy*) which still has some of the original walls in place.

ST KILDA

Scotland's only World Heritage Site, this remote, rocky island some 110 miles (177 km) from the mainland, is owned by the National Trust for Scotland, and co-managed with Scottish Natural Heritage. The village of Hirta was laid out in the 1830s. Corbelled stone structures used for storage and known as 'cliets' are scattered everywhere. In the late 17th century there were about 180 inhabitants, by the 1880s nearly half of the population had emigrated, and the Ministry of Defence had established a base. By 1930 all the remaining inhabitants were evacuated, and today only the army remains in this lonely, inaccessible spot.

SOUTH UIST

South Uist is the second largest island in the Outer Hebrides. With a wonderful 20-mile (32.2-km) stretch of sandy beach in the west, backed by machair, and with mountains sprawling down the eastern side, South Uist is excellent walking country, especially with a pair of binoculars. At Loch Druidibeg National Nature Reserve corncrakes are a frequent seasonal migrant, and there are greylag geese and a good many mute swans further north on Loch Bee. The area is excellent for salmon and trout fishing too.

Lochboisdale, in the south, is the main ferry port. Howmore, about halfway up the island, has the remains of a number of interesting medieval churches. On a circular island in nearby Loch an Eilean stands Caisteal Bheagram, so small a castle that it may possibly have been used as a watchtower, refuge or status symbol rather than as a fortress. Just east of the youth hostel, on what was probably once an island, lie two chapels and two churches, and the burial place of the chiefs of Clanranald, who ruled South Uist from the 1370s. St Mary's, or the Large Church (*Teampall Mor*), was indeed large, by island standards. Near by, to the south, sits Dugal's Chapel (*Caibeal Dubhghaill*). West of St Mary's lies St Dermot's Chapel (*Caibeal Dhiarmaid*), and in the north-east corner Clanranald's Chapel (*Caibeal Chlann'ic Ailein*). Look out for Flora Macdonald's birthplace at Milton and the local museum near by.

PEAT CUTTING

Beds of peat several metres thick have been laid down over thousands of years in the cold, damp, largely treeless and waterlogged areas of the highlands and islands. Temperatures below 5°C ensure that the heathers, mosses and bracken growing there do not decay as in warmer climates, but instead are compressed under their own weight in the absence of oxygen, to produce an organic, rich peat layer which can be burned as fuel for heating and cooking. 'Peats' are cut with special spades in the summer months by the crofters, whose ancient gathering rights are protected under Scots law. The peats are laid out to dry, and then stacked ready for the cold winter months.

The island of Eriskay can be seen off the southern tip of South Uist

The Hebrides

Leisure Information
Places of Interest
Shopping
The Performing Arts
Sports, Activities
and the Outdoors
Annual Events and Customs

Checklist ✓

Leisure Information

TOURIST INFORMATION CENTRES

INNER HEBRIDES
Broadford, Skye
(Seasonal). Tel: 01471 822361.
Portree, Skye
Meall House. Tel: 01478
612137.
OUTER HEBRIDES
Castlebay, Barra
Main Street (Seasonal). Tel:
01871 810336.
Lochboisdale, South Uist
Pier Road (Seasonal). Tel: 01878
700286.
Lochmaddy, North Uist
Pier Road (Seasonal). Tel: 01876
500321.
Stornoway, Lewis
26 Cromwell Street. Tel: 01851
703088.
Tarbert, Harris
Pier Road (Seasonal). Tel: 01859
502011.

OTHER INFORMATION

Ferries
Caledonian MacBrayne Ferries
Ferry Terminal, Gourock. Tel:
01475 650100. For Hebrides via
Firth of Clyde, or west coast
ports; 'Rover' tickets available.
Western Ferries (Clyde) 61
Woodside Crescent, Glasgow.
Tel: 0141 332 9766.

Historic Scotland
Longmore House, Salisbury Pl,
Edinburgh. Tel: 0131 668 8800.
National Trust for Scotland
5 Charlotte Square, Edinburgh.
Tel: 0131 226 5922.
**Royal Society for the
Protection of Birds**
17 Regent Terrace, Edinburgh.
Tel: 0131 556 5624.
Scottish Tourist Board
23 Ravelston Terrace,
Edinburgh. Tel: 0131 332 2433.
Scottish Wildlife Trust
16 Cramond Glebe Road,
Edinburgh. Tel: 0131 312 7765.
Weather
Great Outdoors Weatherline.
Tel: 0891 567538. Mountaincall
for north-west Scotland. Tel:
0891 505680. Weathercall for
north-west Scotland. Tel: 0891
500425.

ORDNANCE SURVEY MAPS

Landranger 1:50,000 sheet
numbers 8, 13, 14, 18, 22, 23,
31, 32, 33, 39.
Outdoor Leisure 1:25,000 sheet
number 8.

Places of interest

There will be an admission
charge at the following places of
interest unless otherwise stated.

INNER HEBRIDES
COLL
Breacacha Castle
Tel: 0187 93444. Open: by
appointment only.
RUM
Kinloch Castle
Boat from Mallaig. Tel: 01687
462037. Tours by arrangement.
SKYE
Aros Heritage Centre
Viewfield Road, Portree. Tel:
01478 613649. Open: Mar–Dec
daily.
**Clan Donald Centre and
Armadale Gardens**
Armadale. Tel: 01471
844305/844227. Open:
Apr–Oct daily.
Colbost Folk Museum
3 miles (4.8 km) west of
Dunvegan. Tel: 01470 521296.
Open: all year daily.
**Croft Museum (Skye
Museum of Island Life)**
Hungladder, Kilmuir. South of
Dunvegan. Tel: 01470 511279.
Open: Apr–Oct most days.
**Dunvegan Castle and
Gardens**
Tel: 01470 521206. Open:
March–end Oct most days.
Kylerhea Otter Haven
North of Kylerhea. Open: all
year daily. Free.
Old Skye Crofter's House
Luib, 7 miles (11.2 km) north

west of Broadford. Tel: 01470 521296. Open: all year daily.
The Piping Heritage Centre
Borreraig, Dunvegan. Tel: 01470 511316. Open: Easter–Oct daily.

OUTER HEBRIDES
BARRA
Cille Bharra
Eoligarry, north end of island. Open: all reasonable times. Free.
BENBECULA
Museum Sgoil Lionacleit
Four miles (6.4 km) south of Baile a'Mhanaich (Balivanich) on B892. Tel: 01870 602211 Ext 137. Open: all year. Free.
Trinity Temple
Off the A865, 8 miles (12.8 km) south west of Lochmaddy. Open: at all reasonable times. Free.
HARRIS AND LEWIS
Black House
Arnol, 15 miles (24 km) north west of Stornoway. Tel: 0131 668 8800. Open: all year most days.
Callanish Standing Stones
Off A858 12 miles (19.2 km) west of Stornoway. Tel: 0131 668 8800. Open: at all times. Free.
Dun Carloway Broch
A858, Carloway. Open: all reasonable times. Free.
Gearrannan Village
A mile (1.6 km) from bridge at Carloway. Open: all year daily.
Museum Nan Eilean
Francis Street, Stornoway. Tel: 01851 703773. Open: all year most days. Free.
Ness Historical Society
Old School, Lionel Ness. Tel: 01851 810377. Open: daily in summer.
Shawbost School Museum
On A858, 19 miles (30.6 km) north west of Stornoway. Open: Apr–Nov most days.
Steinacleit Cairn and Stone Circle
Loch an Duin, 12 miles (19.2 km) north of Stornoway. Tel: 0131 668 8800. Open: all reasonable times. Free.
SOUTH UIST
Flora Macdonald's Birthplace
South Uist. Open: at all reasonable times. Free.

The following places may be of interest to visitors with children. Unless otherwise stated there will be an admission charge.

INNER HEBRIDES
SKYE
Giant MacAskill Museum Centre
Dunvegan. Tel: 01470 521296. Includes a life-size model of Angus MacAskill, Scotland's tallest man at 7 feet 9 inches (2.3 metres) Open: Easter–Oct daily.
Holmisdale House Toy Museum
Glendale. Tel: 01470 511240. Open: all year most days.
Skye Serpentarium
The Old Mill, Harapool, Broadford. Tel: 01471 822209. Open: Easter–Sep most days.

The Performing Arts

INNER HEBRIDES
SKYE
An Tuireann Arts Centre, Struan Road, Portree. Tel: 01478 613306.

Shopping

LOCAL SPECIALITIES

INNER HEBRIDES
SKYE
Distillery
Talisker Distillery, Carbost, on B8009. Tel: 01478 640203.

OUTER HEBRIDES
BENBECULA
Paintings
Studio Gallery, Askernish. Tel: 01878 700237. Open: Apr–Sep most days, at other times by appointment.
HARRIS
Tweed and Shetland Wool
Heather Graham Crafts, Borve Cottage, Borve. Tel: 01859 550202. Open: all year daily.
LEWIS
Pottery
Fear an Eich Coll Pottery, Back. On B895 6 miles (9.6 km) from Stornoway. Tel: 01851 820219.

Sports, Activities and the Outdoors

ANGLING
There are ample opportunities for angling. Enquire at local Tourist Information Offices.

CYCLE HIRE
SKYE
Fairwinds Cycle Hire, Broadford. Tel: 01471 822270.
Island Cycles, The Green, Portree. Tel: 01478 613121.

GOLF COURSES
INNER HEBRIDES
SKYE
Isle of Skye Golf Club. Sconser. Tel: 01478 612341.
OUTER HEBRIDES
LEWIS
Stornoway Golf Club, Lady Lever Park. Tel: 01851 702240.

HORSE-RIDING
SKYE
Skye Riding Centre. Borve. Tel: 01470 532439.
Uig Pony Trekking, Uig Hotel. Tel: 01470 542205.

NATURE RESERVES
Balranald Nature Reserve (RSPB), North Uist
Hougharry. Tel: 0131 556 5624.
Loch Druidibeg National Nature Reserve, South Uist
Call at warden's office. Tel: 01870 620206.

WATERSPORTS:
SKYE
Skye Diving Centre, Dunvegan (Sub-aqua). Tel: 01470 521366.
Whitewave Activities. Uig (Canoeing, windsurfing). Tel: 01470 542414.

Annual Events and Customs

SKYE
Skye Folk Festival, Portree, late July.
Isle of Skye Highland Games, early August.

BARRA
Feis Bharraidh – Isle of Barra Festival, early July.

Ross and Cromarty

The area of Ross and Cromarty sweeps across Scotland, embracing every landscape from the rugged, remote mountains and moorland of Assynt in the west to the rolling, fertile country of the Black Isle in the east. It is noted as a refuge for some of Scotland's native wildlife and as such it has some of the country's finest nature reserves. Ross and Cromarty are also also full of man-made surprises, including the sub-tropical gardens of Inverewe and the spa town of Strathpeffer, a delightful reminder of Victorian prosperity.

ALEXANDER MACKENZIE
In the graveyard of the parish church of Avoch, near Rosemarkie, lie the remains of the great Scottish explorer Sir Alexander Mackenzie (1755–1820). Mackenzie travelled to Canada in 1779 and was soon trading furs for the North West Company, rivals of the more famous Hudson Bay Company. Based at Fort Chipewyan on Lake Athabasca, he set out with a team of Indians in 1789 to discover a route across the continent, but found instead a long river, which would be named after him, leading up to the Arctic Ocean. In 1793 he became the first white man to cross the Rockies and reach the Pacific.

The bulbous hill of Sgurr a'Chaorachain, near the pass of Bealach-na-Ba

APPLECROSS   Highland Map ref NG7144
Looking north from the picture-postcard village of Plockton, the rugged hills of Applecross fill both the view and the imagination. Until the last century this peninsula was almost as isolated as Knoydart. Rough tracks linked the old settlements along the coast down to Toscaig, and access from the south was via the breathtakingly spectacular Bealach-na-Ba, which reaches some 2,050 feet (624.8 metres). In 1965 a road was started around the northern margin from Shieldaig, making a pleasant circular route around this remote and beautiful place.

An Irish saint established a religious community here in the 7th century, but it was destroyed in a Viking raid. Today it is hard to believe that 3,000 people once thrived with their cattle in the green, fertile valley around the quiet village of Applecross itself – cleared from the land when the Mackenzies sold it off for a sporting estate; only the outlines of their deserted cottages remain.

BLACK ISLE Highland

The Black Isle is the fertile spit of land between the Cromarty and Moray Firths. The central forested ridge carries the peninsula's older name of Ardmeanach, and was part of lands gifted to her husband, Lord Darnley, by Mary, Queen of Scots.

Cromarty, on the north-eastern tip of the peninsula, is a delightful 18th-century town, an important centre of fishing and commerce until the 19th century, when it was bypassed by the railways. The whitewashed Court-house Museum ably tells the town's story. Hugh Miller, an eminent 19th-century geologist and writer who started life as a stonemason, lived in the little thatched cottage next door, now in the care of the National Trust for Scotland (see Walk on page 70). The fossil beach where he worked is two miles (3.2 km) away at Eathie.

Fortrose looks out across the Moray Firth. The cathedral was completed in the 15th century, but then unroofed in the 16th, before Cromwell plundered its great sandstone blocks to build the fortifications in Inverness. On the other side of the spit (once a popular spot for witch-burning but now dedicated to golf) lies Rosemarkie, notable for the Pictish remains displayed at the Groam House Museum and Pictish Centre.

The mud-flats of the Beauly Firth attract large numbers of birds – over-wintering greylag and pink-footed geese graze the fields around, and a variety of sea-ducks, including goldeneye and scoter may be seen near the Kessock Bridge.

Evening light catches the impressive ruins of Fortrose Cathedral

DOLPHIN WATCH
Bottlenose dolphins found around the Scottish mainland are some of the largest in the world, and in the Moray Firth area there is one of only two resident populations in Britain, with at least 88 individuals identified. Cromarty has become the best place in Britain to see bottlenose dolphins in the wild – boat trips run by Dolphin Ecosse are available throughout the year (tel: 01381 600323 for details). There are also whale-watching trips during August and September.

Cromarty and the Moray Firth

A walk with excellent views of the Cromarty and Moray Firths, which are only surpassed by sightings of Scotland's only resident group of bottlenose dolphins. Good paths; take a pair of binoculars. The walk can be shortened.

Time: 4½ hours. Distance: 6 miles (9.7 km).
Location: On the A832 at Cromarty.
Start: Park on the large grassy car park area in front of the lighthouse, near the harbour. (OS grid ref: NH787678.)
OS Maps: Landranger 21 (Dornoch, Alness & Invergordon area) 1:50,000.
Pathfinder 134 (Cromarty & Balintore)
Sheet NH 86/87 1:25,000.
See Key to Walks on page 121.

ROUTE DIRECTIONS

Follow the grassy links and pass the fishing quarter and look for a sign for the Courthouse. Turn right up to the Cromarty Arms and the Courthouse, then left past **Hugh Miller's Cottage** to the Cromarty Historic Scottish Kirk. Turn left down Burnside Place, past the Cromarty Study Centre, a converted 18th-century brewery. Turn right at the sign 'South Sutor Viewpoint' along Miller Road, then turn right and go uphill. After the archway on the right, with the sign 'Private House', make a short deviation left to a 17th-century graveyard.

Rejoin the road, heading up to the T-junction where a panorama of Nigg Bay and semi-submersible oil rigs in the Cromarty Firth can be seen. Turn right and then left, passing cottages on to a farm track, and pass through a gate. Walk over the hill to two farm gates. Take the right-hand gate and walk through a wooded glade towards the coast until you see a stile at the bottom on the right.

Dolphins may be seen from here – look out for seagulls hovering over the sea, they may give away their position. From this vantage point you can venture along the top of the cliff, but this is not advisable for children. Descend to the beach with its abandoned fishing huts, sea-stacks and natural arches, but beware of the tide. Return back up the path and over the stile. At this point you can shorten the walk by retracing the path back to Cromarty, or carry on and complete the walk through fields where there may be cattle, including bulls.

To continue, go back to the trees, turn right, go under a fence then walk straight ahead along the edge of the field to link up with the recognised path. At the next fence turn left and walk uphill for 30 yards (27 metres) crossing the right side of the gate on to the grass path around the headland, to another gate and a view of the seven counties/districts of the area: Caithness, Sutherland, Nairn, Ross and Cromarty, Inverness, Moray and Banff. Head downhill on a wide grassy path, through a gap in the fence to a final gate beyond and the Coastguard Lookout Station. Turn left, walk back to Cromarty Mains Farm, then turn right and return to **Cromarty**.

POINTS OF INTEREST

Hugh Miller's Cottage
Built in 1711, the thatched cottage (National Trust for Scotland) is now a museum on the life of Hugh Miller, geologist, writer and editor, who was born here. His numerous books included *Scenes and Legends of Northern Scotland* (1835), and he recorded his findings in palaeontology and geology in *Old Red Sandstone*.

Moray Firth Dolphins
Over 100 bottlenose dolphins have been identified as residing in the Cromarty and inner Moray Firths. Up to 13 feet (4 metres) in length, they can live for 40 years, and are distinguished from porpoises by their grey skin, short noses and playful manner. They use distinctive sounds to communicate with each other, including a unique signature whistle. Harbour porpoises, minke whales, common and grey seals are also prevalent in the area. In 1982, a rare humpback whale was also seen in the central Moray Firth.

Cromarty
The 18th-century seaport town has good examples of

vernacular architecture, with elegant merchants' houses and workers' cottages. Once the harbour was busy exporting salted salmon and importing iron from Russia; today Cromarty has Europe's largest salmon farm.

From the Sutors of Cromarty you can look back to the little town

GRUINARD

For many people, the name of Gruinard is irrevocably associated with the germ warfare tests of World War II, which were to contaminate the land for many years. In a controlled experiment in 1942 a number of bombs containing anthrax were detonated on the little island in the bay, and the results of the bacillus on a flock of sheep were closely observed. Needless to say, the sheep died horribly. Some 45 years later the island was cleaned up and declared safe. Today it is a beautiful, peaceful spot in a magnificent arc of pink sandy bay.

The scattered settlement of Gairloch sprawls along this beautiful coast

GAIRLOCH Highland Map ref NG8076

This popular holiday village with its award-winning Heritage Museum is spread around a sunny, sandy bay, with the heights of the delightfully named Flowerdale looming behind. There are superb views out to the islands, and Gairloch lies at the heart of a fine scenic area which takes in the incomparable Loch Maree. North from the village, the road winds around the bay and eventually turns into a track, leading to the former lighthouse at Rubha Reidh. To the south of the bay there are intriguing woody inlets, perfect for exploring in a small boat. Beyond sheltered Badachro the road passes sandy bays to end at Redpoint, but energetic walkers can take the long path to Diabaig on Loch Torridon.

Behind Gairloch the A832 leads to the long stretch of water that is Loch Maree, famous for its fishing. It is surrounded by high mountains and scattered with darkly wooded islands. The highest peak on the northern shore is Slioch (3,219 feet/981 metres), while to the south Beinn Eighe, with its cap of white quartzite, lies at the heart of Britain's first National Nature Reserve – you can find out about nature trails and picnic spots at the visitor centre at Aultroy, towards the eastern end of the loch. Isle Maree, by Letterewe, was the site of a 7th-century hermitage, and may have had much older, druidical connections. Queen Victoria was enchanted with the whole area when she visited in 1877, giving her name to the waterfall near Talladale.

INVEREWE   Highland Map ref NG8683

Inverewe is further north than Moscow, but, almost seeming to defy nature, is one of the most remarkable of British gardens. In 1862 Osgood Mackenzie crossed peat hags and windswept, treeless moorland, to arrive at this rocky peninsula, jutting into Loch Ewe – and it must have seemed the last place on earth to begin gardening, but a determined gardener is a force to be reckoned with.

First he planted a shelter belt of pines and firs, carted out the rocks and replaced them with hundreds of tonnes of garden soil. Once protected from the winds, Inverewe could benefit from the warming effects of the North Atlantic Drift. Rhododendrons were planted in profusion, and still provide one of the most spectacular attractions in the early summer. Paths meander between them and beneath the pines, and pass an almost bewildering array of rare and exotic plants, collected from all over the world. It would be easy to spend whole days looking at just a few species. Rock gardens are bright with alpines, including many from New Zealand, and in the area called 'Japan' are tree ferns and palms.

There are wonderful views along the loch from the tip of the garden at Cuddy Rock, and also from in front of the house, built in 1937 after fire destroyed Osgood's original building. Near by are an impressive herbaceous border and a more formal walled garden. Around every corner there is surprise and delight. Mackenzie died in 1922, and his daughter Mairi, who had maintained and developed his vision, presented the garden to the National Trust for Scotland in 1952.

Tender plants flourish in the walled garden at Inverewe

FLOWER POTS TO POT SHOTS

Osgood Mackenzie, creator of Inverewe Garden, was a typical Victorian gentlemen when it came to sport. He was a keen shot and proud of his success. In 1856 alone he records bagging 1,900 head of game, including 184 hares, 110 golden plover, 91 rock pigeons, 35 wild duck, 53 snipe and 49 partridges, as well as 1,313 grouse – and this does not include roe deer, ptarmigan, teal and geese. He was anxious to protect his birds from what he called vermin, so he poisoned and trapped foxes, badgers, otters, polecats, pine martens and wildcats. In the course of four seasons he also disposed of 34 golden eagles. Though today we may look askance at such apparently indiscriminate slaughter, Mackenzie was not out of step with his times.

The Ancient Round House of Badachro

A pleasant walk taking in woodland, An Torr and an ancient site. Good views of Loch Gairloch, Badachro harbour and the distant mountains of Wester Ross can be seen before returning along the leafy river's edge. The first section has some uneven ground along the river that is not suitable for very young children or the elderly.

Time: 2 hours. Distance: 2 miles (3.2 km).
Location: 6 miles (9.6 km) south west of Gairloch.
Start: Take the A832 south from Gairloch, turn right at the stone bridge over the River Kerry on to the B8056 signposted 'Red Point and Badachro'. After 3 miles (4.8 km), passing Loch Bad a' Chrotha on the left, pull in and park on the right by the gate and stile just before the old stone bridge.
(OS grid ref: NG785731.)
OS Maps: Landranger 19 (Gairloch & Ullapool area) 1:50,000.
Pathfinder 128 (Loch Gairloch) Sheet NG77 1:25,000.
See Key to Walks on page 121.

ROUTE DIRECTIONS

Go through the gate and follow the steep path above the fast-flowing Abhainn Bad a' Chrotha river. Follow the path downhill (be careful of the steep incline on your left) and at the point where you see a tree-lined island on the other side of the river, turn sharp right, following the path uphill away from the river.

The track then gently ascends on to open moorland with heather and grasses. Near the top of the hill where the path forks, turn right and follow the contours along to the trees. Pass through the birch wood and out on to the heath, covered with heather and cotton grasses. For panoramic views of **Loch Gairloch** and the mountains of Wester Ross, scramble up to the top of An Torr.

Return to the path and follow it downhill sweeping to the left on to a small plain with an ancient circle of stones which are the remains of a **round house** on the right. Return to the path 16 yards (15 metres) from the round house and follow it into the birch woodland and downhill towards the river until you see a gap on the left.

Descend this gully to reach a small rocky outcrop where there is a private and secluded view of sheltered **Badachro Bay** and the old jetty. Retrace your steps and follow the path back through the wood. At the hut circle take the right fork on to the lower path, walk through the **birch woodland** and along the river. In the wet this path can be boggy. Walk upstream, enjoying the views as you return to the starting point.

POINTS OF INTEREST

Loch Gairloch
Gaelic for 'the short sea loch', Loch Gairloch is a popular place for sailing and fishing, although, having said that, it is far from crowded.
The area was once famous for spring cod-fishing. Today, common fish like haddock and mackerel are found here, but the fishermen sometimes catch the more unusual small octopus and cuckoo wrasse. Small boats are available for hire, or there are skippered fishing boats; alternatively, yacht cruises set sail from the nearby harbours.
The Gairloch Heritage Museum is an excellent place to discover the history of the local fishing industry. Exhibits here include two examples of typical fishing boats that have been used in the Loch Gairloch area, both of which are over 60 years old.

Round House 'Hut Circles'
Bronze- and Iron-Age hut circles of this kind are scattered all over Wester Ross. Their roofs were supported by a ring of wooden posts, the walls were likely to have been of made of wicker and the whole structure thatched with some kind of vegetation. Like most south-facing hillside round houses, they were blessed with a superb view.

Badachro Bay
This is a typical Wester Ross fishing village, with an old jetty ramp leading down to the unusually shaped bay and the islands of Eilean Tioram, Sgeir Ghlas and Eilean Horrisdale. The bay is colourful with heather

*Looking over sheltered
Badachro Bay from An Torr*

which reaches down to the
sea shore, where the rocks
are covered with lichen and
fringed with bright orange
seaweed.

Birch Woodland
Wood from the local birch
trees was an adaptable
commodity. It was used to
smoke herrings, build
furniture and make tools
and brooms. Later, before
the invention of plastic, it
was also turned to make
cotton reels. The bark was
useful for tanning and
insulation, and birch was
also turned into charcoal for
iron smelting. The cotton
grass found around
Badachro was traditionally
used for candlewicks and to
stuff pillows.

Gairloch to Ullapool

This is a magnificent 50-mile (80.5-km) linear drive, along the superb mountainous coastline of north-west Scotland, with plenty of viewpoints along the route.

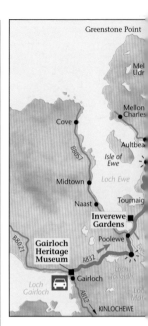

ROUTE DIRECTIONS

See Key to Car Tours on page 120.

The drive starts at the **Gairloch Heritage Museum**, a converted farmstead which depicts the way of life in this West Highland parish, from Stone-Age times to the present day. It includes a Pictish inscribed stone, a reconstructed croft house room, and geology, archaeology, agriculture and fishing sections. From the museum take the A832 signposted 'Poolewe'. Continue on this road passing Loch Tollaidh on the right, until you arrive at magnificent Loch Maree. Pull in at the viewpoint here and admire the scenery.

Drive on, passing through Poolewe – a favourite holiday place – and on to **Inverewe Gardens** some eight miles (12.8 km) from Gairloch. To visit these unique gardens, park in the car park on the left (there are also views of Loch Ewe from here). Inverewe Gardens, owned by The National Trust for Scotland, was created over a century ago by Osgood Mackenzie, and his daughter, Mairi Sawyer, continued the work. Originally a windswept rocky and peaty moorland, with only two small trees, it is now one of Europe's most exotic visual extravaganzas. Taking advantage of its shoreline position and of the Gulf Stream climate, it now has over 2,500 species, including

Himalayan lilies, Japanese hydrangeas, New Zealand shrubs and giant South Pacific forget-me-nots. There is also a peace plot commemorating the end of World War I, a pond garden, a walled garden and Victorian glasshouses.

Continue on the A832, passing on the left a viewpoint from which you can see the Isle of Ewe and an impressive pier and fish tanks on the shore opposite the Island. Continue, passing on the left the minor road to the old crofting townships of Aultbea and Mellon Charles. Continue to Laide and turn left before the garage, toilet and post office to the ruined chapel, believed to have been founded by Columba's monks, and a viewpoint. From here there are magnificent views across Gruinard Bay to Gruinard Island, known for its germ warfare (anthrax) experiments in 1942. The island has since been pronounced clear, and was recently reinhabited.

Return to the main road and continue on the A832 around the bay and over the headland to the viewpoint just before Badcaul, from where there are views over Little Loch Broom to Beinn Ghobhlach and, to the right, the mountain of Sail Mhor. Follow the road along Little Loch Broom, passing rectangular mussel rafts and later fish cages before you reach Ardessie. The square and circular cages are the salt

water stage of the salmon-farming process. At Ardessie you pass a waterfall on the right (Ardessie means high water). Continue, passing the war memorial, to Dundonnell Hotel from where you can see the magnificent tidal salt water flats and abundant wildfowl.

The road now follows the Dundonnell River, which is edged with Scots pine and birch and has a series of lovely waterfalls. The road bears left and on the bend near Sidhean na Sròine is the view of Loch Broom, with lush fields filling the valley floor – reputedly one of the most spectacular roadside views in Scotland. A little further on, at **Corrieshalloch Gorge**, pull in to the car park and go down to the suspension bridge to view the gorge. This is one of the most magnificent sights in the north west; the gorge is a mile (1.6 km) long and 200 feet (60 metres) wide, and has an unusual box canyon. The **Falls of**

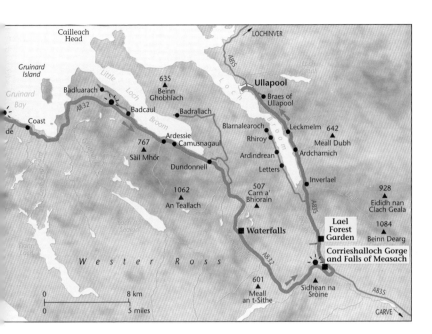

Measach here are 150 feet (46 metres) high.

Continue on the A832 until you reach a T-junction. Turn left here on to the A835(T) towards Ullapool, passing another entrance to the gorge on the left. Continue on the A835, passing **Lael Forest Garden** on your right, descending towards the lush pasture land, with sheep and drystone walls on your left. The road continues with Loch Broom on the left (notice the many crofts on the opposite side of the loch) into Ullapool and the end of the drive. Ullapool, on Loch Broom, is the largest village in Wester Ross and the main ferry link to Stornoway and the Outer Hebrides. In the autumn the loch is full of 'Klondykers' – Bulgarian and Russian factory ships, which follow the mackerel shoals from Shetland.

Rounding the valley at the head of Loch Broom

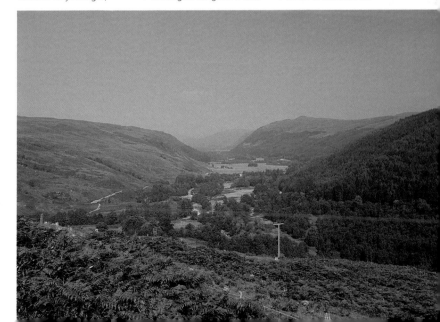

THE CURSE OF CALDA HOUSE
Near the ruins of the
MacLeods' 15th-century
Ardvreck Castle on the shores
of Loch Assynt you can see the
remains of a fine mansion.
This was Edderchalder, or
Calda House, many-
chambered and at least two
storeys high, built around
1720 by the up and coming
Mackenzies. Legend has it
that the unfortunate woman
who lived there was a witch
and had cursed the district in
a fit of rage, so that crops
failed. Around 1737, after yet
another miserable harvest, the
curse was only lifted when the
house was struck by a
righteous bolt of lightning.
Like the house, the castle was
also destroyed by fire.

*From the Knockan Visitor
Centre the distinctive peak
of Suilven can be seen to the
right of Cul Mor*

INVERPOLLY Highland Map ref NC1412

North of Ullapool the habitation is sparse and the
landscape becomes altogether bigger and wilder, with
giant, bare mountains looming out of bleak, bitter
moorland. The Inverpolly National Nature Reserve,
managed by Scottish Natural Heritage, offers access to
this fine, dramatic countryside in all its glory, and the
visitor centre at Knockan is a good place to start. The
diversity of habitats in the region is revealed, including
bogs, lochs and patches of ancient woodland, with a
corresponding diversity of flora. A geology trail here
illuminates the formation of the Assynt area, and part of
the 'Moine Thrust' can be seen in the rocks of Knockan
Cliff. There are excellent views from the top of the
mountains of Coigach. Of these, Stac Pollaidh (2,008
feet/612 metres) is the most popular, and a fairly easy
walk leads up from the minor road by Loch Lurgainn.
Look out for deer and birds of prey, and you may even
see signs of wildcats in the area. To the north on a clear
day you can see the familiar form of Suilven (2,402
feet/732 metres), but this peak is strictly for
mountaineers.

There is a further extensive nature reserve at
Inchnadamph. From here the road leads round the
shores of Loch Assynt, past the ruins of Ardvreck Castle,
where the great soldier Montrose was held prisoner in
1650. Beyond that is the popular angling centre of
Lochinver (this links up with a narrow but very scenic
road from Loch Lurgainn). Up the coast, just north of
the hamlet of Clachtoll, there are the circular remains of
a broch to be seen on the shoreline, dating back to the
first century AD.

SHIELDAIG AND TORRIDON Highland Map ref
NG8154/NG9055

The villages around Loch Torridon are picturesque, but cannot compete with the grandeur of some of the finest mountain scenery in Scotland. The road east from Shieldaig, a whitewashed, 18th-century planned village overlooking the pine-clad Shieldaig Island, gives views over Upper Loch Torridon to the huge mountain mass dominated by what Queen Victoria called 'that extraordinary mountain, Ben Liathach.'

Of red Torridonian sandstone, 750 million years old and 3,339 feet (1,024 metres) high, Liathach has a row of seven peaks topped with shining white quartzite from 150 million years later. It forms part of the National Trust for Scotland's 16,100-acre Torridon Estate. The Trust's Countryside Centre in Torridon village can advise on the best routes in the mountains, but guided walks are recommended if you want to tackle the 5-mile (8-km) ridge between Liathach's peaks.

The Deer Museum nearby has a herd of wild deer, and lots of information about their life on the hills. Further on, Beinn Eighe presents a forbidding face to the traveller, but like the other mountains has impressive corries to the north. Britain's first National Nature Reserve was established here to protect the remnant of the native Caledonian Pine Forest on its slopes.

The road north of Loch Torridon, with wonderful views over to the Applecross peninsula, passes through Fasag, built to house families displaced in the clearances, and several crofting settlements to end at Lower Diabaig, from where you can walk to Redpoint, far out on the coast of Wester Ross.

MOUNTAIN MOGGIES

The hills of Torridon are home to many species, but the wildcats are among the most elusive. They live on the loneliest and most remote mountain sides, hunting at night for small animals and birds, though they have been known to take lambs and young deer, too. Pure-bred wildcats have litters in May, and are bigger than domestic cats, to which they are only distantly related. Their yellowy-grey fur is prominently striped in black, and they have thick, bushy tails. Around 24 inches (61 cm) from nose to tail, they can be awesomely fierce, spitting and growling when roused, though they purr, like any cat, when contented. It is not always easy to recognise a pure wildcat, as so many have interbred with feral domestic cats.

Enjoying an eagle's-eye view to the red ridge of Liathach, high above Torridon village

The charming old Pump Room is a reminder of Strathpeffer's glorious heydays

VITRIFIED FORTS

Vitrified Iron-Age hill forts are found throughout Scotland, Ireland and continental Europe. Vitrification occurred when the wooden beams used in the construction of stone ramparts were set on fire by an attacking enemy – the intense heat could cause certain softer rocks to melt and re-fuse in great lumps on cooling. Knock Farril, above Strathpeffer, is a particularly good example; another is Craig Phadrig, set on a prominent hilltop to the west of Inverness.

STRATHPEFFER Highland Map ref NH4858

Once hailed as 'the Harrogate of the North', Strathpeffer is a curious phenomenon to find above the Highland line – a genteel, attractive little spa town, complete with Victorian architectural twirls such as verandahs and ornamental barge-boards. Locals had known about the curative properties of the mineral springs here for centuries, but thanks to the serious scientific analysis of the water in 1819, Strathpeffer became a boom town. The first pump room opened the following year, and visitors flocked to fill the new hotels and villas. While never perhaps in the same league as Bath, the town did attract royalty from overseas, and the railway had to be specially extended from Dingwall to cater for the number of visitors – at the height of its fame there were through-trains from London, and the 'Strathpeffer Express' direct from Aviemore.

Inevitably, tastes changed, and Strathpeffer's popularity declined after the war. The spa buildings have disappeared, and the old wooden railway station now houses crafts and visitor centres, but the Pump Room remains, and the town offers excellent golfing and recreational facilities to its visitors. Don't miss the Pictish stone slab, set in a field near the station. Deeply carved with an inverted, patterned horse-shoe shape above a standing eagle, its original purpose is unknown.

There are several good places to walk here, including the ridge of Knock Farril to the south (see Walk on page 82), and through the woods to the Falls of Rogie to the west. Salmon may be seen in the Blackwater River here, and there are pleasant picnic sites between the trees.

ULLAPOOL Highland Map ref NH1294

As you approach on the A835, the little whitewashed town of Ullapool is neatly laid out before you on a spit of land curving into the waters of Loch Broom. The tidy grid-plan of the streets reveals that this is a model town, and indeed it was laid out to a plan developed by the British Fishery Society in 1788. The site was carefully chosen to provide a good harbour for the fishing, and to squeeze out the Dutch herring vessels which had been taking full advantage of the lack of local boats. The great Thomas Telford had a hand in the design, but the herring did not last, and, without the lifeline of the railway, the settlement declined. The Fishery Society had chosen their site well, however, and in the first half of the 20th century boats came over from the east coast and fortunes revived. Today the great hulks of factory ships, or 'Klondykers', from eastern Europe anchor in the sheltered waters of Loch Broom, processing mackerel and helping to keep the local economy afloat.

Tourism is also important – Ullapool is the gateway to the remote north-western tip of Scotland, as well as the main ferry port for Stornoway. The broad streets are well worth exploring – there's a good little museum, and you could treat yourself to dinner at the famous Altnaharrie Inn across the loch (via the Inn's own launch; advance booking essential). Around the coast at Achiltibuie is the Hydroponicum, a scientific delight, where bananas and other exotic plants thrive without the benefit of soil – it is open through the summer, and seeing is believing! At the head of Loch Broom, don't miss the dramatic Corrieshalloch Gorge, and the suspension bridge just below the Falls of Measach.

THE SUMMER ISLES

This little group of islands lies just off the coast, some 12 miles (19.3 km) north west of Ullapool, and are well worth a visit if you enjoy peace and quiet – seals and seabirds are the chief inhabitants.

Naturalist Fraser Darling lived on Tanera More and wrote his *Island Years* here. Today, fish-farming has replaced fish-curing as the main support for the islands.

Ullapool was carefully planned out in the 18th century

Knock Farril Fort and The Eagle Stone

A spectacular walk to a vitrified fort, views of Loch Ussie and a fine Pictish stone. A gentle hill climb on clear paths.

Time: 3½ hours. Distance: 5 miles (8 km).
Location: Strathpeffer.
Start: From the Tourist Information Centre in Strathpeffer drive up the hill and turn left in front of the youth hostel; drive down the wooded lane, turn sharp left at the parking sign and park in the car park. (OS grid ref: NH481573.)
OS Maps: Landranger 26 (Inverness & Strathglass Area) 1:50,000.
Pathfinder 159 (Dingwall & Strathpeffer) Sheet NH 45/55 1:25,000.
See Key to Walks on page 121.

ROUTE DIRECTIONS

The entrance to **Blackmuir Wood** is marked by a brown post with coloured bands, and a sign directing you to the **Touchstone Maze**. Go through the ranch-style gate into the forest, keeping left at every junction, and follow the sign 'Forest Walk'. Follow posts with green and blue bands until you see fields on the left. Cross a plank bridge. On the left is a stile of two half logs and a path leading down the field – remember this point for the return journey.

Follow the sign to the Touchstone Maze. Keeping the maze on your right, follow the path uphill until it intersects a broad path; turn left and keep straight ahead. Go through the gate at the end of the forest and continue until the path divides, taking the right track which swings uphill on to a flat area between the ridges.

Turn left up towards the grass-covered ruins of **Knock Farril Fort**, and the magnificent views of Dingwall, the Cromarty Firth and stands of old Scots pine. Return to the flat area beneath the fort. Do not follow the original path, but head uphill over the facing hog's-back ridge for views of Loch Ussie and Strathpeffer.

At the end of the ridge go through the gate and turn sharp right downhill to a very broad path. Cross over this path and continue downhill through a small clearing to the next path. Turn left, and after about 66 yards (60 metres), turn right down to the Touchstone Maze and along to the stile referred to earlier in this walk. Cross over the stile into the field, keeping left, until a steep road takes you to the Ben Wyvis Hotel.

Follow the signs for the Symbol Stone (**Eagle Stone**), cross the road (A834), turn left, then right and continue until you reach a leafy lane. Halfway down the lane turn left through a gap in the hedge to see the Pictish stone and the distant view of Knock Farril. Go back down the lane and return to the main road. Turn right and walk past the Museum of Childhood, the Spa Tea Room and the Tourist Information Centre. Follow the road through **Strathpeffer** uphill to the Youth Hostel, turn left and return to the car park.

POINTS OF INTEREST

Blackmuir Wood
Managed by the Forestry
Commission, the wood
contains mostly conifers,
but also birch, rowan and
bird cherry.

Touchstone Maze
Although a modern
construction, dated 1992,
the maze was built

incorporating alignments
with the sun and moon,
with a labyrinth pathway. It
is constructed from all the
major rock types of the
Highlands and Islands of
Scotland, with a display to
identify them, and includes
the Lewisian rocks of the
Outer Hebrides and west
coast which are over 3,000
million years old.

Knock Farril Fort
This Iron-Age fort
(800–500BC) is the best
example of a vitrified fort in
the north of Scotland.
Vitrified literally means
'turned to glass', and was a
process by which the fort
walls were strengthened by
adding wood between the
stones then setting fire to
the main structure, which
produced a blast furnace
effect, melting the rocks and
fusing them together. The
result resembles slag with

*Strathpeffer lies cradled in a
rolling green valley, seen
here from the ridge of Knock
Farril*

distinctive bubbles and flow
marks.

**The Eagle Stone (Symbol
Stone)**
The 7th-century Pictish
stone with a carved eagle is
possibly a memorial to a
chief, a territorial marker or
a symbol of a marriage
alliance. The stone's name
Clach an Tiompan, means
'sounding stone' or 'stone
on the ground'. Local
folklore suggests that if the
stone falls over three times
the valley floor will flood.

Strathpeffer
Britain's most northerly spa
town, Strathpeffer's first
pump room was built in
about 1820, after sulphur
and chalybeate springs were
discovered. Hordes of
visitors descended on the
town from as far afield as
London, after a pavilion, a
rheumatic hospital and
hotels were established.

Ross and Cromarty

✓ Checklist

Leisure Information

TOURIST INFORMATION CENTRES

Gairloch
Auchtercairn. Tel: 01445 712130.
Glenshiel
(Seasonal.) Tel: 01599 511264.
Lochcarron
Main Street (seasonal). Tel: 01520 722357.
North Kessock
Tel: 01463 731505.
Strathpeffer
The Square (seasonal). Tel: 01997 421415.
Ullapool
West Shore Street (seasonal). Tel: 01854 612135.

OTHER INFORMATION

Ferries
Caledonian MacBrayne Ferries. Ferry Terminal, Gourock. Tel: 01475 650100. For Hebrides via Firth of Clyde, or west-coast ports; sailings to 23 islands. 'Rover' tickets available.
Forest Enterprise
Forestry Commision, 231 Corstorphine Road, Edinburgh. Tel: 0131 334 0303.
Historic Scotland
Longmore House, Salisbury Place, Edinburgh. Tel: 0131 668 8800.

National Trust for Scotland
5 Charlotte Square, Edinburgh. Tel: 0131 226 5922.
Royal Society for the Protection of Birds
17 Regent Terrace, Edinburgh. Tel: 0131 556 5624.
Scottish Tourist Board
23 Ravelston Terrace, Edinburgh. Tel: 0131 332 2433.
Scottish Wildlife Trust
16 Cramond Glebe Road, Edinburgh. Tel: 0131 312 7765.
Weather
Great Outdoors Weatherline. Tel: 0891 567538. Mountaincall for north-west Scotland. Tel: 0891 505680. Western Highlands, Climbing line – 5 day forecast. Tel: 0891 200819. Weathercall for north-west Scotland. Tel: 0891 500425.

ORDNANCE SURVEY MAPS

Landranger 1:50,000 sheet numbers 15, 16, 19, 20, 21, 24, 25, 26, 33, 34.
Outdoor Leisure 1:25,000 sheet number 8.

Places of Interest:

There will be an admission charge at the following places of interest unless otherwise stated.
Achiltibuie Hydroponicum
Achiltibuie. 26 miles (41.8 km) north west of Ullapool. Tel: 01854 622202. Robert Irvine's garden of the future, growing plants without soil. Open: Easter–Sep daily. Tours at 10am, 12noon, 2pm, 3.30pm and 5pm.
Countryside Centre
North of Torridon, off A896. Tel: 01445 791221. Audio-visual presentation on scenery and wildlife. Open: centre late Apr–early Oct; estate and deer museum all year daily.
Cromarty Courthouse
Church Street, Cromarty. Tel: 01381 600418. Open: Easter–Oct daily.
Gairloch Heritage Museum
Gairloch. Tel: 01445 712287. Open: Easter–Sep most days; Oct–Mar by arrangement.
Groam House Museum and Pictish Centre
High Street, Rosemarkie. Tel: 01381 620961. Open: May–Oct most days.
Hugh Miller's Cottage
Church Street, Cromarty. Tel: 01381 600245. Open: end Apr–early Oct most days.
Inverewe Gardens
On A832 at Poolewe, 6 miles (9.6 km) north east of Gairloch. Tel: 01445 781200. Open: all year daily. Visitor Centre and shop Apr–Oct daily.

Leckmelm Shrubbery and Arboretum
On A835, 3 miles (4.8 km) south of Ullapool. Tel: 01854 612356. Open: Apr–Sep daily.
Lochbroom Museum
Captain's Cabin, Quay Street, Ullapool. Tel: 01854 612356. Open: May–Sep most days.
Ullapool Museum
7–8 West Argyll Street. Open: late Mar–early Nov most days.

SPECIAL INTEREST FOR CHILDREN

The following places may be of interest to visitors with children. Unless otherwise stated there will be an admission charge.

Houses in the tidy little village of Shieldaig all face a tree-covered island

Black Isle Wildlife and Country Park
Drumsmittal, North Kessock. Tel: 01463 731656. Open: Mar–Nov daily.
Highland Museum of Childhood
The Old Station, Strathpeffer. Tel: 01997 421031. Open: Apr–Oct most days.

Shopping

LOCAL SPECIALITIES

Cheeses
Highland Fine Cheeses, Shore Road, Blarliath, Tain. Tel: 01862 892034. Conducted tours and tastings.
Crafts
Highland Line Craft Centre, in the centre of Achnasheen, by the railway station. Tel: 01445 720227. Open: Apr–Oct daily; winter by arrangement.

Distilleries
Glen Ord Distillery Visitor Centre, off the A832 on the outskirts of Muir of Ord. Tel: 01463 871334. Guided tours. Open: Jan–Dec weekdays only; restricted hours Dec–Feb.
Glenmorangie Distillery Visitor Centre, 1 mile (1.6 km) from Tain on the A9 towards Wick. Tel: 01862 892477. Tours daily, or by appointment.
Haggis
George Cockburn and Sons, 19 Mill Street, Dingwall. Tel: 01349 862315.
Smoked Products
Achiltibuie Smokehouse, at Altandhu, 5 miles (8 km) west of Achiltibuie, north west of Ullapool. Tel: 01854 622353. Open: Easter–Oct weekdays only, but also Sat in high season.
Stoneware
Highland Stoneware, Mill Street,

Ullapool. Also at Lochinver. Tel:
01571 844376 (Lochinver);
01854 612980 (Ullapool).

Sports, Activities and the Outdoors

ANGLING

There are ample opportunities
for angling of all kinds in the
area. Enquire at local Tourist
Information Offices.

BOAT TRIPS

Moray Firth
Dolphin Ecosse. Tel: 01381
600323. Trips to see Dolphins; 2
hours duration. Must be booked
in advance. Also whale-watching
trips Aug–Sep.
Summer Isles
Cruises from Achiltibuie. Tel:
01854 622200/622315. Rock
formations, seals and bird-life.
Ullapool Islander Cruises. Tel:
01854 612385. Summer Queen
Cruises. Tel: 01854 612472.
Safari Nature Cruises. Tel: 01854
612129.

COUNTRY PARKS, FORESTS AND NATURE RESERVES

**Beinn Eighe National Nature
Reserve**
Kinlochewe. Tel: 01445
7602544.
**Inverpolly National Nature
Reserve**
At Knockan Cliff, off the A835,
12 miles (19.2 km) north east of

Ullapool. Open: May–Sep most
days.
Lael Forest Garden
On the A835 south of Ullapool.
Two signposted car parks.
Various waymarked walks
through the forest with a forest
garden of interesting trees from
Britain and abroad.
Torridon Estate
Tel: 01445 791221. A 114,000-
acre reserve in the Torridon Hills.

CYCLING

Contact Dornoch Forest
Enterprise. Tel: 01862 810359,
or Easter Ross Forest Enterprise,
Hilton of Embo, Dingwall Tel:
01349 62144.

GOLF COURSES

Alness
Alness Golf Club, Ardross Road.
Tel: 01349 883877.
Fortrose
Fortrose Golf Club, Ness Road
East. Tel: 01381 620529.
Gairloch
Gairloch Golf Club. Tel: 01445
712407.
Lochcarron
Lochcarron Golf Club, East End.
Tel: 01520 722257.
Muir of Ord
Great North Road. Tel: 01463
870825.
Portmahomack
Ten miles (16.1 km) east of Tain
off the A9. Tel: 01862 87236.

*Finding time for a relaxed
picnic in spectacular Glen
Torridon*

Tain
Tain Golf Club, Golf Links. Tel:
01862 892314.

HORSE-RIDING

Dingwall
Seaforth Riding Centre,
Maryburgh by Dingwall. Tel:
01349 865495.
Tain
Northwilds Riding Centre,
Fendom by Tain. Tel: 01862
892468.

WATERSPORTS

Muir of Ord
Fairburn Activity Centre
(canoeing). Tel: 01997 433397.

Annual Events and Customs

Fortrose
St Boniface Fair, mid August.
Dingwall
Highland Traditional Music
Festival, late June/early July.
Dingwall Highland Games, mid
July.
Muir of Ord
Black Isle Show, early August.
Plockton
Plockton Regatta, late July to
early August.

Caithness and Sutherland

The wide expanses of central Sutherland form one of the few wilderness areas remaining in western Europe, and their conservation is a matter of worldwide concern. Moor, bog and mountain support a rich diversity of plantlife which can be studied at the heart of the Flow Country, or at the extreme geographical points of Cape Wrath and Dunnet Head. Settlement is mostly confined to the coastal areas, with the fishing communities of the west, pleasant holiday places such as Golspie and historic towns like Thurso.

BETTYHILL   Highland Map ref NC7061

Lying beside a rocky bay on Scotland's inhospitable, wave-bashed northern coast, the village of Bettyhill is linked for ever with the infamous Elizabeth, 1st Duchess of Sutherland, whose name it bears. With her husband and the hated factor, Patrick Sellar, the Duchess was prominent in the clearing of Sutherland's fertile land, evicting tenant crofters and replacing them with sheep. The scheme caused great hardship across the Highlands, and many were forced to emigrate in the clearances of 1814 and 1819. The green valley of Strathnaver, which runs south from Bettyhill to Syre and south west to Altnaharra, once supported some 64 clachans and little townships; today it is eerily deserted. The Strathnaver Museum, east of Bettyhill, tells of those times and of the families who scraped a living along this wild shore.

Beside the road to Skelpick is a chain of prehistoric burial mounds, and Farr churchyard contains a carved slab cross from the 9th century. Today people come for the fishing and the landscape, or to trace the history of their dispossessed forebears.

THE UNQUIET GRAVE

In the churchyard at Farr you must look hard to find the fallen obelisk which commemorates the Reverend David MacKenzie. MacKenzie was the Duchess's man, given the unenviable task of serving the first eviction notices in 1814, and later assuring her ladyship that her tenants were happily resettled after the burning of their homes, despite evidence of great hardship and suffering. MacKenzie attempted to make amends in a letter to the estate in 1818, but his life was tainted, and his tomb is said to be cursed, for the stone will not stay upright. Old memories die hard in the Highlands.

The inhospitable shoreline at Farr, by Bettyhill

A TALE OF TWO BRIDGES

Today a bridge carries the A9 safely over the narrows of the Dornoch Firth, but until recently travellers relied on a boat to carry them between Ferrytown and Ferry Point on Cambuscurie Bay. Tragedy struck one night in 1809 when the ferry, overladen with revellers fresh from the market at Tain, capsized and sank; 70 lives were lost. The causeway bridge on the A9 north of Dornoch, across the head of Loch Fleet, replaced an old ferry crossing in 1815, and was designed by the great Thomas Telford.

Dornoch boasts an attractive little cathedral

DORNOCH   Highland Map ref NH8089

At the wide mouth of the Dornoch Firth, the dignified town of Dornoch is a popular holiday resort with great beaches, a lively craft centre and a world-class championship golf course. The modern course is described as 'very challenging', but golf has been taken seriously here since 1616, when monks from the local community started playing. In a garden down by the links stands the Witch's Stone, marking the demise of the unfortunate Janet Horne in 1722, who was tarred and feathered before being burned at the stake for turning her daughter into a pony and other devilish practices.

A royal burgh, the town was formerly important as the seat of the Bishops of Caithness – their castle is now a comfortable hotel. The tiny 13th-century cathedral was caught in the crossfire of a clan feud and burned down in the 16th century. It was finally rebuilt around 1835, with funds provided by the unpopular Elizabeth, Duchess of Sutherland. At Skelbo, north of Dornoch, a good forest walk takes you past the remains of an ancient broch.

DURNESS Highland Map ref NC4067

The odd little settlement of Durness is about as far as you can drive into the wild north-west corner of Scotland, but it is not quite the end of the road. The hamlet of Balnakeil lies a bit further north on the fertile Faraid peninsula and marks the site of the former radar station which was abandoned in the 1960s. Taken over by the local community, the old prefabricated buildings now contain a crafts centre. Gaelic scholars may come in search of the grave of the 18th-century poet Rob Donn, and golfers may fancy a game on the mainland's remotest golf course, but most visitors are drawn here by the lure of Cape Wrath. To visit the cape you must catch the summer ferry from neighbouring Keodale and take a minibus across the desolate, boggy moorland (the Royal Navy use it as a firing range) to reach the top. There's not a lot to see there, except a lonely lighthouse perched high on the cliffs, but chill winds and the roar of the pounding waves remind you that there are only the Faroe Islands between you and the Arctic. On a clear day you can see for miles from this point – as far as the Outer Hebrides and even Orkney. Britain's highest cliffs are along here, at Clo Mor (918 feet/280 metres), and offshore stacks support a famous colony of gannets.

Between Durness and the long, deep inlet of Loch Eriboll, Smoo Cave is well worth exploring. The name 'Smoo' derives from 'Smuga' – a hole or hiding place. A steep path leads down to the cavern, where the high arched mouth opens into three great chambers. There are watery pools within the cave, and dripping limestone has created a Gothic collection of stalactites and stalagmites. Sir Walter Scott started the tourist trail here in 1814, when the cave could only be approached from the sea.

The gaping mouth of Smoo Cave is approached today by a long flight of steps

WHAT'S IN A NAME?
The dramatic, angry seas hitting the reefs and cliffs around Cape Wrath suggest that this most north-westerly point of Britain is particularly well named. However, Wrath is probably taken from the Norse word 'hvarth', a turning point, and would have been a significant landmark on Viking raiding routes around the coast. For pilots and seafarers it is still a familiar turning point, though thoughts of the wrath of the sea can never be far away.

Rosal Clearance Village, Sutherland

Starting alongside the River Naver, famous for its salmon, the clearly marked path through the forest leads to Rosal Clearance Village, which played an important, but tragic, part in Scotland's history. An easy walk on a well-signposted path.

Time: 1¼ hours. Distance: 2¼ miles (3.6 km).
Location: 12 miles (19.2 km) south of Bettyhill.
Start: From the Clearance Museum in the Old Church at Bettyhill take the A836 south. Turn left on to the B871 signposted 'Syre 9 miles'. Cross over the bridge at Syre and turn immediately right on to the Forestry Commission track signposted 'Naver Rosal Pre-Clearance Village'. After a mile (1.6 km) turn left into the car park. (OS grid ref: NC691427.)
OS Maps: Landranger 10 (Strathnaver) 1:50,000.
Pathfinder 64 (Mid Strathnaver) Sheet NC64/74 1:25,000.
See Key to Walks on page 121.

ROUTE DIRECTIONS

Go through the safety gate and follow the flat wide track through the Naver forestry plantation of Scots pine, **lodgepole pine** and larch planted in the early 1960s. Cross the Allt Rosail, a small stream, pass a large creosoted shed with a felt roof and continue until you reach the sign to **Rosal Village**. Turn left into a clearing in the centre of the forest, then go right and over the duck-boards. The first cairn describes the clearance of the Rosal township which was excavated by Glasgow University. Go through the gate and follow the white arrows. The walk depicts the life of the pre-clearance inhabitants through a series of interpretative boards.

Continue uphill to the next cairn which describes the traditional long houses which were built of stone, peat bog pine and heather. Follow the path to the boards describing the people, their animals and their crops, and pass a souterrain (an underground chamber) cairn of graded stones. Walk over marshy ground on duck-boards and

stepping stones to the cairn, the highest point on the site, and the echo point. Enjoy the panorama then turn around to face the forest and shout into the trees to find the natural 'echo' which bounces back off Beinn Rosail (853 feet/260 metres).

Continue on, now downhill, and fork left to a cairn at the edge of the forest. Follow the path which now bears to the right along the boundary fence, walk past huts and into the forest again. Leave by the safety gate and follow the green sign for the car park, turn right uphill (not left, the way you came in). Keep on this path through the forest; three types of deer are found here, including red deer, the largest native land mammal in Britain. Walk past fire breaks and follow the green signs with white arrows to the car park. Near the stream in tube culverts, look right where there is a small waterfall. Notice the lichen on the pine trees here, also the mosses and bracken. Follow the path as it curves down to the left. The River Naver comes into

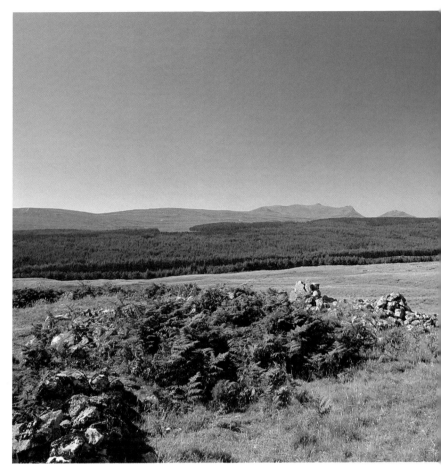

view, and you return to the starting point.

POINTS OF INTEREST

Lodgepole Pine

Extensively planted on peat bogs throughout Scotland, lodgepole pine is said to be used for the poles of North American wigwams, hence the name 'lodgepole', and occurs naturally from California to Alaska.

Rosal Village

Rosal Village stands as a monument to the tragic history of the Scottish Clearances. It was emptied of its inhabitants in 1814 by landowners, who cleared the villages to make way for Cheviot sheep and increased profits. This system of monoculture, with its bigger and heavier sheep, destroyed the local agriculture and the heather. In its place bracken and rushes took hold of the land. The terrible events of the evictions, by gangs of men burning houses and destroying families, is brought tragically alive in Donald MacLeod's *Gloomy Memories*, a response to the book *Sunny Memories – A Visit to Dunrobin* by Harriet

All-smothering forestry has taken over from the sheep which replaced the people of Strathnaver

Beecher Stowe. It was written as an apologia for the Sutherlands, who were responsible for the most vicious evictions in the Highlands and Islands. Around 15,000 people were cleared from the Sutherland estates. MacLeod himself suffered eviction with his wife. He wrote about the harrowing events, including some around Rosal, near where he was born.

THE FLOW COUNTRY Highland

Over half of Caithness and Sutherland is covered by a
great swathe of blanket bog – The Flow Country (from
the Old Norse, *Flói,* meaning marshy ground). Until very
recently it was a landscape which had more or less
escaped the attention of human hands. Over a period of
some 7,000 years peat accumulated at a very slow rate,
often not more than a millimetre per year, reaching a
depth of between 16 and 23 feet (5–7 metres).

The Flow Country is not only unique, but is a natural
resource of global importance – a complex mosaic of
peat bog and dark, peat-stained pools. Viewed from the
ground its almost primeval appearance can't be fully
appreciated, but from the air the true beauty, remoteness
and expansiveness of the area is quite breathtaking. The
barren appearance is deceptive – the area is of immense
wildlife importance, with sphagnum moss forming the
living skin of the bog, dotted with sundews, sweet
scented bog myrtle, heaths and heather.

It is for its birds, though, that it is so very special,
particularly the breeding waders, many of which are
declining in numbers globally because of the loss of
suitable habitats. The Flow Country supports around 70
per cent of the European Community's breeding
population of greenshank, together with 20 per cent of
the black-throated diver and other species such as dunlin
and golden plover. In the dimming light of dusk there
are few more evocative and thought-provoking
experiences than to hear the plaintive 'wheep' of the
golden plover or the hauntingly mournful cry of the
black-throated diver.

Very few roads traverse this great expanse of land and
there are only rare signs of human habitation. Forsinard,
which lies on the A897, is little more than a hotel and a
railway station. The former must be one of the remotest
in Scotland and the station is an ideal destination for
more adventurous walkers.

GOLSPIE AND HELMSDALE Highland Map ref
NC9004/ND0215

Golspie and Brora are two delightful little resort towns
on the east coast, midway between Inverness and Wick,
offering lovely sandy beaches and facilities for sailing,
golf and other holiday pastimes. On the wooded hill
behind Golspie stands a statue of the 1st Duke of
Sutherland. The 2nd Duke was embarrassed here in 1854
when he tried to raise troops to fight in the Crimea – his
listeners heard him out before politely reminding him
that his family's preference for sheep had depopulated
the land, and that nobody could – or would – be spared
for fighting.

Just up the coast stands the absurdly turreted
Dunrobin Castle. Remodelled by the Victorian architect
Charles Barry to resemble a French château, it actually
dates back to the 13th century, and is the seat of the

Dukes of Sutherland. The castle has served in its time as both a naval hospital and a school. The gardens, modelled on Versailles, are particularly splendid. Beyond Brora, just before the turning at Lothbeg, look out for a stone at the roadside which commemorates the last wolf to be killed in Sutherland.

Set on the coast where the River Helmsdale enters the sea, the little fishing town of Helmsdale has found itself at the centre of several gold rushes over the years. The settlement grew up reluctantly in the 19th century as crofters, cleared from the Strath of Kildonan, were forced to take up herring fishing to survive. The award-winning Timespan Heritage Centre tells this story and much more, from the arrival of the Picts and the Vikings to the discovery of offshore oil.

GOLD FEVER

When alluvial gold was found in the tributaries of the River Helmsdale in 1868, a mini gold rush ensued. While hardly on Klondike scale, the field had yielded £12,000-worth of gold by 1870. You can still pan for gold here. Ask at Strath Ullie Crafts and Fishing Tackle in Helmsdale.

Dunrobin's extraordinary exterior belies a more venerable heart

The Last House Museum draws the tourists to John o'Groats

DUNNET HEAD

The beetling sandstone cliffs at Dunnet Head, 407 feet (124 metres) high, are a good two miles (3.2 km) further north than John o'Groats, and therefore rightly claim to be the northernmost point of mainland Britain. The lighthouse on the clifftop, built by Robert Stevenson, looks out over the turbulent waters of the Pentland Firth, a familiar hazard to sailors, where the Atlantic Ocean meets the North Sea. Windsurfing championships have been held round the corner in the broad, sandy sweep of Dunnet Bay.

JOHN O'GROATS   Highland Map ref ND3872

On summer days the tour buses churn into the village at John o'Groats, and churn out again laden with souvenirs. This is not actually the most northerly point on the British mainland at all, but years of publicity – thanks to the eccentrics who walk up here from Land's End to raise money for charity – have drawn the tourists here. It's an arduous route, some 870 miles (1,400 km) or longer depending on your choice of path, and the cheerful white-painted hotel at the end must have been a very welcome sight for many a weary, foot-sore traveller. The Last House Museum gives an interesting account of the area.

On a clear day you can see northwards beyond the little island of Stroma to Orkney. Dutchman Jan de Groot operated the ferry to South Ronaldsay at the end of the 15th century and gave his name to the settlement – you can find memorials to his family in the old church at Cannisbay, to the west. Her Majesty Queen Elizabeth, The Queen Mother, attends the church here when in residence at her Scottish home, the Castle of Mey (not open). To the east lies Duncansby Head, with a lighthouse and a good walk south along the high cliffs to see the tall stacks of rock just offshore, home to thousands of noisy seabirds, including puffins and cormorants.

There have been various plans over the years to turn John o'Groats into a more serious tourist centre, perhaps along the lines of the controversial complex at Land's End, but these have never quite materialised.

LAIRG AND LOCH SHIN Highland Map ref NC5806
Great expanses of Sutherland are devoid of any human
habitation, the result of the now infamous Clearances in
the late 18th century and first half of the 19th century.
One of the few remaining townships is Lairg, lying at the
southern end of Loch Shin – a vast expanse of fresh
water, 24 miles (38.4 km) long and on average a mile
(1.6 km) wide.

Stretching away to the north is a pleasant if not
dramatic landscape of mountains, moor, lochans and
streams which occasionally tumble down as waterfalls.
Towards Altnaharra, a tiny village in the middle of
nowhere but a Mecca for salmon anglers, the landscape
is dominated by the towering presence of Ben Kilbrech,
which rises to 3,153 feet (961 metres).

Lairg has been described as the 'Rome of Sutherland',
the place to which all roads lead, and it is a place of
considerable social and economic importance to the
surrounding area. In August each year there is a one-day
sale of sheep – as many as 250,000 may change hands,
making it easy to believe that every sheep in the region
is there on that day.

There is much to see and admire around Lairg,
including plenty of evidence of earlier habitation in hut
circles, a broch at Sallachy on the southern shore of Loch
Shin and a number of Neolithic stone circles and cairns.
The cairn at The Ord just outside Lairg has been
excavated and is well worth a visit.

The hydro-electric scheme at the southern end of Loch
Shin controls the flow of water in the River Shin, but
salmon are still able to make their way up to the
spawning redds. At the right time of year you can watch
them leaping up the Falls of Shin, a couple of miles
downstream from Lairg, where specially constructed
viewing platforms are provided.

A PLAID TOO FAR
It is an irony of Scottish
history that tartan, that proud
and colourful emblem of a
nation, recognised with
sentimental warmth across
the world, did not reach its
fullest potential until the
commodity of wool became
more widely available. Of
course, as sheep-farming took
over the land, so the Scots
were forced off it.

Tartan – the cloth of many
colours woven in formal
patterns of checks and stripes
– emerged as a potent symbol
of clan identity at the end of
the 16th century. By the 18th
century patterns had been
refined into 'setts', but
proscription after the 1745
uprising resulted in the
destruction of many records.
Today the tartan industry
thrives on a spirit of Scots
kinship, with new patterns
and colourways to suit
modern fashion, and its
application to every Scottish
souvenir you could imagine.

*The small township of Lairg
is famous for its annual
sheep sales*

PUFFINS
Of all the seabirds familiar around the northern coast of Scotland, the rotund puffin is one of the favourites. With their big, brightly coloured bills and red feet, puffins are easily recognised, and while the biggest breeding colony is on inaccessible St Kilda, their burrows are also to be found at many other points around the coast in cliffs and on grassy slopes. July is probably the best month to observe these comical little birds, but you may see them any time between March and August.

SCOURIE Highland Map ref NC1544

The village of Scourie lies on the shores of Edrachillis Bay, and thanks to the warm air of the Gulf Stream this is the northernmost point in Britain where Atlantic palm trees will grow – you can see them growing in the gardens of Scourie House. This was the home of General Hugh Mackay, born here in 1640, who was a Covenanter and soldier, rising to become commander-in-chief in the Highlands. Linked with events at Killiecrankie and Cromdale, Mackay is credited with the invention of the offset bayonet.

Scourie is a popular centre for walkers and anglers, and especially with birdwatchers who come in early summer to visit the nature reserve on nearby Handa Island. Handa once supported as many as seven families, ruled by their own 'queen' – traditionally the oldest widow. The last islanders were driven away in the 1840s when the potato harvests failed, and today the birds reign supreme on the cliffs – thousands of wheeling gulls, guillemots, kittiwakes, puffins and razorbills. In the care of the Scottish Wildlife Trust, Handa can be reached by boat from just up the coast at Tarbet.

East of Scourie, the River Laxford, crossed by the A838 at Laxford Bridge, is noted for its salmon, and there are numerous lochans to explore in this wild landscape. The hills here are rugged lumps of Torridon sandstone – inland, Foinaven 2,979 feet (908 metres) and Arkle 2,579 feet (786 metres) gave their names to famous racehorses. Continue north up the A838 and turn off for Kinlochbervie to see a busy fishing port in action. This road ends at Shegra, but you can walk on to enjoy the delights of beautiful, secluded Sandwood Bay.

THURSO Highland Map ref ND1168

After travelling across the vast empty expanse of Sutherland it is somehow surprising to arrive at such a thriving little town on the north coast. The Vikings were probably the first to spot the potential of this location, where a good salmon river pours through a long, narrow harbour and into the bay. Orkney can be glimpsed across the stormy waters of the Pentland Firth, and is reached via the ferries which leave from nearby Scrabster.

Thurso developed not so much as a fishing port, but rather a bustling centre for trade, especially with Scandinavia. Meat, fish and notably grain from Caithness were exported with such success that the town's system of weights was adopted as the standard for Scotland. Local flagstones were shipped around the world. With the fall in trade the town might have died, but fortunes revived with the building of the Dounreay nuclear power station, which is now a key employer – the visitor centre has been refurbished and is well worth a visit.

Thurso's prosperous history is reflected in its wide main streets and pleasant squares. Look out for royal coats of arms over various doorways – Her Majesty Queen Elizabeth, The Queen Mother, shops here. It is also worth visiting the heritage museum in the Town Hall. The curiously dignified shell of St Peter's Church dates from the 12th century. Later restored, it was finally abandoned in the 19th century and now stands open to the skies. The statue of Sir John Sinclair (1745–1835) commemorates the great agriculturalist, who pioneered many new ideas in northern Scotland. There is a portrait of him, by Raeburn, in the Scottish National Portrait Gallery in Edinburgh, which shows a tall man dressed determinedly in tartan 'trews' – he apparently considered them more authentic and practical than the kilt.

'THE FOUNDER'

William Smith was born in Pennyland House, on the western outskirts of Thurso, in 1854, the son of a former dragoons officer. Brought up in Glasgow from a young age, he became an active member of the Free College Church and of the Lanarkshire Volunteers. Embracing the Victorian spirit of 'muscular Christianity', he founded the Boys' Brigade in 1883 for 'the advancement of Christ's Kingdom among Boys', an organisation which gave predominantly urban boys a sense of discipline, purpose and Christian brotherhood. More regimental than the Boy Scouts, which started later, it is still going strong today.

The empty shell of old St Peter's lies near the centre of Thurso

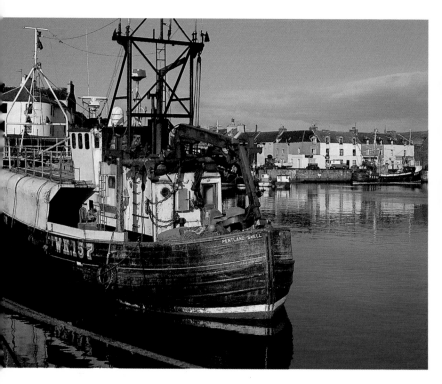

Fishing boats at rest in the harbour at Wick

FLAGSTONES

Underlying much of Caithness is a grey, thinly bedded, carbonate-rich siltstone. This has been widely exploited in the area, the thin layers of stone cut and polished as flagstones, which can be seen everywhere as paving, roofing and even forming walls. Flagstones quarried at Castleton were exported from Thurso during the 19th century, and appear all over the world, from London's Euston Station to Melbourne, Australia. The industry was finally elbowed out by the more convenient pre-cast concrete, but some flagstones are still quarried here.

WICK   Highland Map ref ND3650

Traditionally locked into rivalry with Thurso, the town takes its name from the Norse word for a bay, *vik*, and the oldest part lies to the north of the river. To the south, Pultneytown was laid out by Thomas Telford for the British Fisheries Society in the early 19th century. With its substantial harbour, the timing was just right to take advantage of the herring glut. The town prospered, its numbers swelled by migrant workers from western Scotland and Ireland. The curing yard and old photographs at the heritage centre recall Wick's heyday, when the harbour bristled with fishing boats.

Today's invaders are probably in search of bargains at the Caithness Glass factory shop, but older times brought the Vikings, and the imposing castle of Old Wick dates from those violent days. More ruined forts litter the northward coast. Castles Girnigoe and Sinclair stand side by side on Noss Head; an over-eager Sinclair heir was incarcerated in the former for seven horrible years before apparently dying of starvation and 'vermin'. A couple of miles west is Ackergill Tower, remodelled in the 19th century. At the top of Sinclairs Bay, near the remains of two Iron-Age brochs, 16th-century Keiss Castle stands on the precipitous cliff edge. A more comfortable Baronial-style replacement was built inland in the 19th century.

Caithness and Sutherland

Leisure Information
Places of Interest
Shopping
The Performing Arts
Sports, Activities and the Outdoors
Annual Events and Customs

Checklist

Leisure Information

TOURIST INFORMATION CENTRES

Bettyhill
Clachan (seasonal). Tel: 01641 521342.
Dornoch
The Square. Tel: 01862 810400.
Durness
Sango (seasonal). Tel: 01971 511259.
Helmsdale
Coupar Park (seasonal). Tel: 01431 821640.
John o'Groats
County Road (seasonal). Tel: 01955 611373.
Lairg
(Seasonal.) Tel: 01549 2160.
Lochinver
Main Street (seasonal). Tel: 01571 844330.
Thurso
Riverside (seasonal). Tel: 01847 892371.
Wick
Whitechapel Road. Tel: 01955 602596.

OTHER INFORMATION

Ferries
Caledonian MacBrayne Ferries Ferry Terminal, Gourock. Tel: 01475 650100. For the Hebrides via the Firth of Clyde, or the many ports on the west coast with sailings to 23 islands. Two excellent value 'rover' tickets are offered.
P & O Scottish Ferries Jamiesons Quay, Aberdeen. Tel: 01224 572615. Daily sailings to Orkney from Scrabster (Thurso). Sailings from Orkney (Stromness) to Shetland (Lerwick). Also sailings from Aberdeen.
Forest Enterprise
Forestry Commision, 231 Corstorphine Road, Edinburgh. Tel: 0131 334 0303.
Historic Scotland
Longmore House, Salisbury Place, Edinburgh. Tel: 0131 668 8800.
National Trust for Scotland
5 Charlotte Square, Edinburgh. Tel: 0131 226 5922.
Royal Society for the Protection of Birds
17 Regent Terrace, Edinburgh. Tel: 0131 556 5624.
Scottish Tourist Board
23 Ravelston Terrace, Edinburgh. Tel: 0131 332 2433.
Scottish Wildlife Trust
16 Cramond Glebe Road, Edinburgh. Tel: 0131 312 7765.

Weather
Great Outdoors Weatherline. Tel: 0891 567538. Mountaincall for north-west Scotland. Tel: 0891 505680. Western Highlands, Climbing line – 5 day forecast. Tel: 0891 200819. Weathercall for north-west Scotland. Tel: 0891 500425.

ORDNANCE SURVEY MAPS

Landranger 1:50,000 sheet numbers 9, 10, 11, 12, 15, 16, 17, 20, 21.

Places of Interest

There will be an admission charge at the following places of interest unless otherwise stated.
Ardvreck Castle
On the A837 by Loch Assynt. Built in 1490, now a ruin. Always open. Free.
Cape Wrath
Twelve miles (19.2 km) north west of Durness. The most northerly point of Scotland's north-west seaboard. Passenger ferry (summer only) connects with minibus service to the Cape. Ferry: Tel: 01971 511376. Mini bus: Tel: 01971 511287/ 511343.

Castles Girnigoe and Sinclair
Noss Head. 3 miles (4.8 km)
north of Wick. Ruined clifftop
castles. Always open. Free.

**Clan Gunn Heritage Centre
and Museum**
Latheron, Helmsdale. 16 miles
(25.7 km) south west of Wick.
Tel: 01593 721325. Open:
Jun–Sep most days.

Dounreay Exhibition Centre
On the A836 west of Thurso.
Tel: 01847 802121, ext 2702.
Open: mid May–Sep, exhibition
open most days, but advance
booking required. Free

Dunbeath Heritage Centre
Old School, Dunbeath. Tel:
01593 731233. Open:
Easter–Oct daily.

**Dunrobin Castle and
Gardens**
One mile (1.6 km) north east of
Golspie on A9. Tel: 01408
633177. Open: Easter and
May–mid Oct daily.

Flagstone Trail
Castlehill, Castleton, A836, 4
miles (6.4 km) east of Thurso.
Tel: 01847 821256. Original
source of flagstones exported
worldwide. Outside trail

showing quarrying, stone-
dressing and harbour from
which the flagstones were
exported.

Grey Cairns of Camister
Five miles (8 km) north of
Lybster, Wick. Tel: 0131 668
8800. Megalithic cairns. Near by
are the Clyth stone rows and
Achavannich Stone Circle.
Always open. Free.

Lhaidhay Croft Museum
On the A9 just north of
Dunbeath. Tel: 01593 731244.
Open: Easter–mid Oct daily.

Northlands Viking Centre
On the A9, Quoys of Reiss, Wick.
Tel: 01955 603761. Traces the
Norse settlement of Caithness.

Orcadian Stone Company
Main Street, Golspie. Tel: 01408
633483. Exhibition of local
geology; also fine mineral
specimens from all over the
world. Charge for museum.
Open: all year most days.

Smoo Cave
Durness. Contact Durness
Tourist Information Centre. Tel:
01971 511259. Vast limestone
caves. Open: all reasonable
times. Free.

Strathnaver Museum
Bettyhill. Tel: 0164 521418.
Open: Apr–Oct most days.

**Strath Ullie Crafts and
Fishing Tackle**
Dunrobin Street, Helmsdale.
Contact Mr Sangster. Tel:
01431 821343. Panning for
gold in Kildonan Burn, 9 miles
(14.4 km) from Helmsdale. The
shop hires out gold-panning
equipment, and gives advice
on the best places to try your
luck and how to go about it.
Open: all year most days.

Thurso Heritage Museum
Town Hall, High Street, Thurso.
Open: Jun–Sep most days.

Timespan Heritage Centre
Dunrobin Street, Helmsdale. Tel:
01431 821327. Open:
Easter–Oct daily.

Wick Heritage Centre
20 Bank Row, Wick. Tel: 01955
605393. Open: Jun–Sep most
days.

*The magnificent curving
sweep of Dunnet Bay has
proved popular with wind-
surfers*

SPECIAL INTEREST FOR CHILDREN

The following places may be of interest to visitors with children. Unless otherwise stated there will be an admission charge.

Fossil Visitor Centre
Village Hall, Spittal. On the A895 south of Thurso. Tel: 01847 841266. Open: Jun–Sep certain days.

Highland and Rare Breeds Farm
Elphin, on the A835 14 miles (22.5 km) north of Ullapool. Tel: 01854 666204. Open: mid May–Sep daily.

Kingspark Llama Farm
Berriedale, north east of Helmsdale. Tel: 01593 751202. Open: all year daily.

Rare Breeds Farm and Visitor Centre
Choraidh Croft, on the A838, 10 miles (16.1 km) south east of Durness. Tel: 01971 511235. Open: May–Oct daily. Admission is free for accompanied children.

Shopping

LOCAL SPECIALITIES

Crafts
Dornoch Craft Centre, Town Jail, Dornoch. Tel: 01862 810555. Tartan weaving and exhibitions. Wooden Ewe, Dunnet, John o'Groats. Tel: 018470 85765. Studio and shop.

Distillery
Clynelish Distillery, on the northern outskirts of Brora. Tel: 01408 621444. Open: all year weekdays only.

Glass
Caithness Glass Factory and Visitor Centre, Airport Industrial Estate Wick. Tel: 01955 602286. Viewing gallery and exhibition. Free.

Pottery
Sutherland Pottery, Shinness, north west of Lairg on the A838. Tel: 01549 402223.

Weaving
Ousdale Weaving, Berriedale, 7 miles (11.2 km) north of Helmsdale on the A9. Tel: 01431 821371. Open: Easter–Oct daily; Nov–Easter weekdays only. Free.

The Performing Arts

Lyth Arts Centre
Between Wick and John o'Groats. Tel: 01955 641270. Art exhibitions and touring dance performances. Entrance charge for adults, free for children. Open: Apr–Sep daily.

Sports, Activities and the Outdoors

ANGLING

Fly
Dornoch Lochans Fishery. Tel: 01862 810600.
For further information on angling, enquire at local Tourist Information Centres.

BOAT TRIPS

Enard Bay
Badnaban Cruises. South of Lochinver. Tel: 01571 844358. Small boats to seal and bird colonies in Enard Bay.

Loch Glencoul
Statesman Cruises. A894 over Locha Chairn Bhain. Kylesku Bridge. Tel: 01571 844446. Boat cruises up Loch Glencoul to Eas Coul Aulia waterfall.

Loch Laxford
Laxford Cruises. Fanagmore, 3 miles (4.8 km) north of Scourie. Tel: 01971 502409. Pleasure cruises to see birds, otters, dolphins, seals and whales.

Smoo Cave
Cape Sea Tours, boat trip to Smoo Cave, and to see local wildlife. Contact Durness Tourist Information Centre.

COUNTRY PARKS, FORESTS AND NATURE RESERVES

Handa Island Nature Reserve
Three miles (4.8 km) north west of Scourie. Seabird sanctuary with guided walks. Small open ferry from Tarbet, 4 miles (6.4 km) north of Scourie, for boat trips.

GOLF COURSES

Bonar Bridge
Bonar Bridge Golf Club. Tel: 01549 421248.

Brora
Brora Golf Club, Golf Road. Tel: 01408 621417.

Caithness
Halkirk. Achalone Activities. On the B874, 7 miles (11.2 km) from Thurso. Tel: 01847 831326.

Dornoch
Royal Dornoch, Golf Road. Tel: 01862 810219.

Durness
Durness Golf Club. A mile (1.6 km) west of Durness. Tel: 01971 511364.

Golspie
Golspie Golf Club, Ferry Road. Off A9 half a mile (0.8 km) south of Golspie. Tel: 01408 633266.

Lybster
Lybster Golf Club, Main Street. (No telephone number.)

Reay
Reay Golf Club. Tel: 01847 811288.

Thurso
Two miles (3.2 km) west of Thurso. Tel: 01847 811288.

Wick
Wick Golf Club. Signposted on the A9 north of Wick. Tel: 01955 602726.

GUIDED WALKS

Hidden Hills
Kintradwell, 4 miles (6.4 km) north east of Brora. Private estate with guided wildlife walks. Tel: 01431 831264. Bookings also through Helmsdale Tourist Information Centre. Tel: 01431 821640.

HORSE-RIDING

Thurso
Achalone Activities, Halkirk, Caithness. On the B874 8 miles (12.8km) from Thurso. Tel: 01847 831326.

Wick
Lyth Riding Stables. Crossroads, Lyth. Tel: 01955 641318.

Annual Events and Customs

Thurso
Caithness Highland Gathering and Games, early July.

The Northern Isles
ORKNEY ISLANDS

The 90 or more islands and skerries of the Orkney Islands are like a handful of emeralds cast on the waters of the North Atlantic, their gentle, green, undulating landscape in sharp contrast to the rugged scenery of the north mainland of Scotland. There is a sensation of space, with never-ending skies and great expanses of ocean. Time has not stood still, but there is a timelessness here which is difficult to describe but impossible to ignore. The 20th century arrived with the North Sea oil industry, but reminders of a long history are all around, from evocative standing stones and other great prehistoric monuments, through great buildings such as Kirkwall Cathedral, to the Italian Chapel and the silent sentinels of World War II gun emplacements.

THE BA' GAME

This twice annual event, held at Christmas and New Year, probably originated in rivalry between the youths of two parts of the town when Kirkwall was granted the Scottish Royal Charter in 1486. In its present form, the game has been played since around 1850. The 'Uppies' play the 'Doonies', with team members' allegiance decided by birthplace – 'up or doon the gate'. Up to 200 'players' may be involved – the Doonies have to get the ba' to the sea (normally Kirkwall harbour); the Uppies' goal is the junction of Main Street and New Scapa Road. At the end of the game an individual winner is named by popular acclaim, and as such the title is regarded as a great honour.

KIRKWALL   Map ref HY4411

The first reference to Kirkwall is as *Kirkjuvagr*, Old Norse for Church Bay, which appears under the date 1046 in the great Norse saga *The Orkneyinga Saga*. Kirkwall never gained prominence as a great sea port, but nevertheless became an important settlement which grew rapidly with the building of the cathedral. Much remains of the old town which developed between the 16th and 18th centuries, with narrow winding streets and lanes and compact houses, often with their gable ends on to the street. Above all, St Magnus' Cathedral dominates the town and it is the centrepiece of a rich collection of fine architecture dating from the 12th to 17th centuries.

St Magnus' Cathedral is one of only two intact pre-Reformation cathedrals in Scotland. Built of local red and yellow sandstone, it is a building of magnificent robustness which from the outside gives no indication of the wonderful feeling of space and tranquillity inside. Earl Rognvald started the building in 1137; he was the nephew of Earl Magnus, who had been murdered by his own cousin, Earl Haakon, some 20 years earlier and whose bones are contained within the massive north choir pillar. The cathedral was not completed, however, until sometime in the 15th century.

Clustered around the cathedral are the ruins of the Bishop's Palace, dating from between the 12th and 16th centuries, and the Earl's Palace (1606), which has been described as the most mature and accomplished piece of Renaissance architecture left in Scotland. The main entrance, the oriel windows and the great fireplace in the hall are particularly outstanding features. Tankerness House (1580), now a museum, was originally occupied by the clergy of the cathedral and later acquired and added to by the Baikies of Tankerness, wealthy merchants of that time.

MAES HOWE   Map ref HY3313

Maes Howe stands in a field at the south end of the Loch of Harray, near to the A965, the main road between Stromness and Finstown. The massive chambered cairn, dating from around 2800BC is one of the great treasures of the art of the prehistoric European mason. The mound itself is almost 115 feet (35 metres) in diameter and 23 feet (7 metres) high, surrounded by a low bank and ditch. The inner chamber is nearly 15 feet (4.5 metres) square, lined by beautifully fitting stone slabs with a corbelled roof, with three side chambers built into the walls. You enter through a passage over 47 feet (14.5 metres) long and nearly 5 feet (1.4 metres) high, lined by huge stone slabs, the largest of which is estimated to weigh more than three tonnes. The interior of the tomb is awesome, and we can only wonder at the forces and beliefs that drove these people to undertake a project of this scale with such skill and dedication.

Inevitably it was broken into and the contents plundered many centuries ago, but the structure has survived more or less intact. The loss of the contents can never be fully compensated for, but the Norsemen who broke in and sought shelter from a great storm here have left a magnificent legacy of Runic inscriptions, together with other stone carvings, including a walrus, a serpent knot and a dragon.

STANDING STONES

There are a great many standing stones in the Orkney Islands, mostly monoliths or pairs, but including the two great circles of Ring of Brodgar and the Stones of Stenness. Of all the stone monuments in Orkney, the Ring of Brodgar is the most evocative. Originally a perfect circle of 60 stones, only 27 are still standing. Such construction by Neolithic people represents a massive commitment. Experts have estimated that the excavation of the ditch around the Ring of Brodgar would have taken some 80,000 man-hours to dig, even before the stones themselves were cut, transported and erected. The wonder of these massive monuments is all the greater for the mystery which still surrounds their true purpose.

The grassy mound of Maes Howe conceals an ancient burial chamber

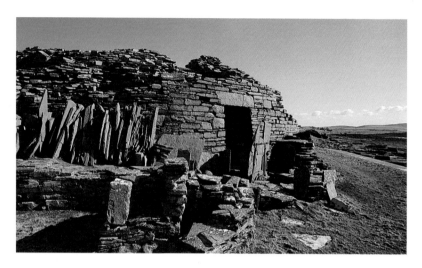

Midhowe broch stands exposed on a promontory

ISLAND WILDLIFE
The northern islands are a wildlife paradise. The cliffs, maritime heaths, moorlands, freshwater lochs, beaches and sea are home to a range of birds. The elusive corncrake can still be heard, if not seen, on Papa Westray, and many other birds visit in the summer to breed, including red-throated divers, Arctic terns, Arctic skuas, great skuas, fulmars and kittiwakes, along with various auks. The maritime heath supports a rich flora, including heath spotted orchid, spring squill with its profusion of delicate sky blue flowers, and both the primrose and Scottish primrose, *Primula scotica*. The seashores around the islands range from exposed rocky headlands to sheltered sandy bays, and support a wide range of wildlife. Common and grey seals are to be seen, and otters also frequent the shore, but are more wary of human company and more difficult to see.

ROUSAY AND OTHER ISLANDS

The 15 main northern islands of Orkney have names to conjure with – Eynhallow (Holy Isle), Eday (Isthmus Isle), Wyre (Spearhead Isle) and Sanday (Sandy Isle). Each has a unique character and a particular contribution to make to the history and culture of the Orcadians, such as the collecting of cast kelp, or 'tangle', or the North Ronaldsay breed of sheep which have evolved to graze the seaweed on the shore and cannot digest grass.

All the islands are worth visiting, either by ferry or by air (flights include the shortest scheduled air route in the world, taking less than 2 minutes for the 1½-mile/2.4-km hop between Westray and Papa Westray). Many of the island air strips are simply fields, making the most exciting part of the flight the avoiding of cow pats on landing and take off!

Rousay, across Eynhallow Sound from the mainland of Orkney, is one of the largest of this group. Its two high points are Blotchnie Fiold (820 feet/250 metres) and Kierfa (771 feet/235 metres), and the climb is rewarded by panoramic views of the islands. Rousay has been inhabited for at least 5,000 years and all around are chambered cairns, brochs, Viking sites and medieval ruins. On an island littered with relics, Midhowe Cairn and Midhowe Broch, overlooking Eynhallow Sound, stand out. Midhowe Cairn, from the 3rd millennium BC, is one of the finest examples of a chambered cairn so far discovered. The remains of 25 people were unearthed during the excavations, including nine complete skeletons. The broch, occupied between 200BC and 200AD, is built on a promontory, with outer defences on the landward side. Artefacts found here included some of Roman origin, bone and stone spindle whorls and evidence of both iron and bronze workings.

SCAPA FLOW AND HOY

The sheltered waters of Scapa Flow were an important naval anchorage in the two World Wars, and are famous for the sinking of HMS *Royal Oak* by the German submarine *U47* in 1939. This prompted the construction of the Churchill Barriers – a great causeway littered with blocks of concrete, linking Mainland to the islands of Lamb Holm, Glimps Holm, Burray and South Ronaldsay, cutting off access by sea from the east. Italian prisoners of war worked on the Barriers and created their own extraordinary monument – the Italian Chapel on Lamb Holm, converted from two Nissen huts. The craftsmanship and faith which have so evidently gone into the chapel's decoration leave you with a sense of deep admiration for human ingenuity.

Drive across the Barriers, down the eastern chain of islands, and you will find that they typify the lush farmland of Orkney. Unlike the rest of Orkney, however, there is a dearth of archaeological relics. A notable exception is the chambered cairn on South Ronaldsay, known as the 'Tomb of the Eagles'. Around 340 people were buried here over a period of some 800 years up to 2200BC, but the name comes from the skeletons of sea eagles also found there.

Hoy (Old Norse *Ha-ey*, meaning 'high land') forms the south-west boundary to Scapa Flow, and of all the Orkney Islands this is most like the Highlands of Scotland, with heather moor supporting a range of sub-Arctic and alpine plants together with a wide variety of birds. There are marvellous opportunities for vigorous walks, and those who make it to the top of Ward Hill (1,555 feet/477 metres) or Cuilags (1420 feet/433 metres) will be rewarded with fabulous views of the Flow and the other islands. In the valley between Ward Hill and the Dwarfie Hammars lies the Dwarfie Stane, a unique chambered cairn, hollowed out of a slab of sandstone using only stone implements.

THE GERMAN FLEET

Scapa Flow was home to the Royal Navy in both World Wars, but even their presence could not rival the sight of the German High Seas Fleet which was escorted to Scapa Flow in 1919 after the surrender of Germany at the end of World War I – 74 vessels in all, including battleships, battle cruisers and destroyers.

On 21 June 1919 the entire fleet was scuttled by their skeleton German crews on receipt of the order 'paragraph eleven' from Admiral Reuters. Many vessels have since been salvaged, but 12 remain on the sea bed of Scapa Flow, including the battleships *Kronprinz Wilhelm*, *Markgraf* and *König*. These vessels, although in relatively deep water, are now a great attraction for visiting scuba divers.

The steep purple hills of Hoy are seen clearly from the mainland

A glimpse of prehistoric life is caught in the ancient dwellings of Skara Brae

THE PEOPLES OF ORKNEY

Little is known about the first settlers of Orkney, around 6,000 years ago, but burial sites around the islands offer a tantalising clue to a culture that honoured their dead. The Picts arrived in around 700BC, and even less is known about them, although they too have left monuments in the form of brochs. Christianity arrived in the 5th century and soon after that came the golden age of the Vikings, whose legacy was the most lasting. Many island place-names are derived from Old Norse, and architectural feats include St Magnus' Cathedral and the the Brough of Birsay settlements. It wasn't until the 13th century that the Orkney Islands became a part of Scotland – as part of the dowry of Margaret of Denmark on her marriage to James III of Scotland.

SKARA BRAE Map ref HY2318

The remains of the Neolithic settlement of Skara Brae are now almost at the high water mark and, if it wasn't for the protection of a sea wall, they would be seriously threatened by erosion. When it was inhabited, between 3100BC and 2500BC, the village was separated from the sea by sand dunes and a freshwater loch. The dunes eventually swallowed up and covered the site until 1850, when a great storm swept away enough of the sand to show the presence of stone structures. Further excavation revealed this to be a priceless piece of Orcadian archaeological heritage, giving a remarkable glimpse of domestic life in earlier centuries.

Over the 600 years that the settlement was inhabited, rebuilding and modification took place, but what you see today are six remarkably similar rectangular houses linked together by narrow winding passages, all embedded in a surrounding midden (now tastefully grassed over). Each house has a central hearth, small cells or cupboards recessed into the walls, slab-built beds, a stone dresser, and clay-lined stone boxes sunk into the floor. The entrances are small, and could be barred and secured from the inside. The roofs would have been of turf and animal skin, laid over driftwood and whalebone. Broken pottery, chert tools and jewellery found here suggest that there would have been as many as 50 people living at Skara Brae at any one time. We can only wonder about the lives those early settlers may have led – on a fine summer's day it seems almost idyllic, but in midwinter no-one would envy the rigours they must have endured.

STROMNESS Map ref HY2508

The sea has always been the life blood of Stromness, situated on the safe and sheltered shores of Hamnavoe, and it remains so to this day – the ferry, the *St Ola*, runs between here and Scrabster on the Scottish mainland. The over-riding importance of the sea to the early residents of Stromness is apparent in that most of the earliest houses are at the sea edge, gable end on, and each has its own pier or slipway. You get a good impression of this from the windows of the splendid Pier Arts Centre. If this is the first impression of most visitors, the second is of the main street through Stromness – a narrow, winding, paved and cobbled road.

Before the advent of regular Atlantic voyages, Stromness was little more than a hamlet – there were just 21 houses and shops here in 1792. That was before the Arctic whaling industry and trade with Canada (particularly the Hudson Bay Company) sparked its growth to over 500 homes by 1841. The full story is told in the excellent Stromness Museum.

Visiting vessels brought prosperity to Stromness, their last stop before Greenland or America (the great explorers Captain Cook and Sir James Franklin were among them). They needed large quantities of provisions for their voyages, including fresh water from Login's Well, which can still be seen. Sometimes the vessels also took on crew, and for a time the narrow streets provided ideal hunting grounds for the Royal Navy press gangs. Shipping activity reached its peak with the herring boom of the late 19th and early 20th centuries – at its peak there could be over 400 boats in and around Hamnavoe – but by 1907 it was all over, the stocks of herring exhausted by over fishing. The same thing, of course, is still happening in the world today – different fish, but the same greed and short-sightedness.

ORKNEY WHISKY

Orkney has two working distilleries, the most northerly in Scotland. Until 1920 there were three, but the 'Old Orkney' distillery in Stromness fell victim to the Temperance Movement which gained such support in the town that it was 'dry' between 1920 and 1947. The Highland Park Distillery, on Holm Road on the outskirts of Kirkwall, was established in 1825, just two years after distilling was legalised. It is one of the few distilleries which still malts its own barley, feeding the four stills which produce an aristocratic 12-year-old whisky with a unique smoky, silky texture. There is an excellent reception centre, and conducted tours are available. The Scapa Distillery lies across Scapa Bay. It was established in 1885 and its pair of pot stills produce a distinctively smoky, salty dram which is aged for eight years in Bourbon casks.

Older houses crowd the inner harbour at Stromness

On average, Fair Isle endures 64 days a year of winds exceeding 34 knots, and gusts of 64 knots (hurricane force) are not uncommon. Combine this with the vagaries of the currents and the fog which can roll in to envelop the island and you have a sure recipe for shipwrecks. Little is known of those which occurred before the 19th century – with the notable exception of the *El Gran Grifon*, a troop ship of the Spanish Armada which foundered there in 1588. In 1868 a German migrant ship, the *Lessing*, was wrecked, but the courage and seamanship of the islanders saved all 465 people, who were taken off the stricken vessel in the local long, narrow rowing boats known as yoles. Lighthouses at each end of the island were commissioned in 1892, but still the wrecks continue.

The isolated island of Fair Isle is owned by the National Trust for Scotland

FAIR ISLE AND FOULA

Between them, Fair Isle (Old Norse *Fridarey* – 'truce island') and Foula (Old Norse for 'island of birds') are two of Britain's loveliest and remotest inhabited islands and yet few people have been privileged to visit them, despite links by both air and sea between Shetland and Fair Isle. Fair Isle lies almost equidistant between Orkney and Shetland, some 25 miles (40.2 km) to the south of Sumburgh Head – to many people just a dot in the ocean which deserves a mention on the shipping forecasts. Foula lies 14 miles (22.5 km) to the west of Shetland, its precipitous sandstone cliffs rising to towering heights of 1,220 feet (372 metres).

FAIR ISLE

There are a number of good reasons for visiting Fair Isle, not least the prehistoric remains near Funniquoy Hill and Vaasetter, and the remains of an Iron-Age fort at Landberg. The Haa House, dating from around the 18th century, was where Sir Walter Scott stayed when he visited the island in 1814. Archaeological records show that the island has been inhabited since before 1000BC. It has a ruggedly beautiful coastline of steep cliffs rising to around 590 feet (180 metres) at their highest, interspersed with stacks, arches and caves sculpted by the continuous erosion by the unrelenting weather and waves. The sea surrounding Fair Isle, known as The Roost, is infamous for the roughness of its troubled waters at the meeting of the contrary currents of the Atlantic Ocean and the North Sea.

Most of today's human visitors come to admire the spectacular scenery and birdlife for which Fair Isle is famous. It was in recognition of the great importance of Fair Isle, both as a stop-over for migrating birds and as a breeding site, that George Waterston established what is now an internationally renowned bird observatory. By the end of 1988, over 340 species of bird had been recorded, and of those only 35 were resident or regular summer breeding species. Fair Isle can boast no fewer than 17 'new for Britain' records and a further 15 'new for Scotland' ones.

In the spring the birds are all in their finest breeding plumage and you are treated to vivid displays such as the bluethroats, with their startling blue bibs with a scarlet spot. Autumn is the time to see the rare and unusual visitors, and each year the list of species is different. The majestic sea cliffs are also ideal for a whole range of breeding seabirds. Of the 24 species which regularly breed in Britain, 17 occur on Fair Isle, amounting in total to around 90,000 pairs. At the height of the breeding season the cliffs and sky are a blizzard of birds – various auks, Arctic and great skuas, terns, gannets, common gulls and storm petrels to name but a few. It is a spectacle which has to be seen (and heard) to be believed.

FOULA

As the summer sun sinks slowly in the western sky, framing the distinctive, ragged outline of Foula in a fiery backdrop of reds and golds, it creates a truly memorable image. Life on Foula has always been a remote and isolated existence and, despite the improved ferry service to mainland Shetland and an air service, the people of Foula still live in the past – literally. It is one of the few places left in Europe, if not the world, to observe the old Julian Calendar, which means that Christmas Day is celebrated on what is 6th January to the rest of us, and New Years Day falls on 13th January!

Crofting, fishing and spinning and weaving provide the main source of income for the islanders, although tourism is increasing, particularly among those who crave peace and solitude. Visitors come here both to appreciate the beauty of the land and seascapes and to study the wildlife. There are superb opportunities to observe seabirds – 18 species breed here, including puffins, guillemots, razorbills, fulmars, storm petrels and Leach's petrels, together with the largest and densest colony of great skua anywhere in the world.

Sunset over Foula, from
Eshaness

FOULA DAYS

The Julian Calendar was a solar rather than lunar dating system, established by Julius Caesar on the advice of the Alexandrian astronomer, Sosigenes. The year was 365¼ days long, divided into 12 months, each with either 30 or 31 days, except February which had 28 days or 29 days in leap years. It sounds familiar, but Sosigenes had made a miscalculation, overestimating the length of the year by 11 minutes 14 seconds!

By the mid-16th century the seasons had shifted by about 10 days. Pope Gregory III ordered a reform of the calendar in 1582, which advanced the date by 10 days. The only difference between the calendars is that no century year is a leap year unless exactly divisible by 400. Further fine tuning states that any year evenly divisible by 4,000 should not be a leap year, and this ensures that the Gregorian Calendar remains accurate to 1 day in 20,000 years.

THE NORTHERN LIGHTS
Undoubtedly the greatest light-show on earth, the Northern Lights (*Aurora Borealis*) are a not infrequent sight in Shetland on clear winter nights, although they are predominantly a phenomenon of the high latitudes. Great shimmering lights ranging in colour from pure violet white through the whole spectrum to red can be seen on occasions, and no two shows are the same. They are the product of solar flares which send charged particles hurtling through space, only to discharge their energy as light in the upper atmosphere. They must have seemed a very strange and mysterious spectacle to the ancient peoples living on the islands, and may well have been the source of the mythological Valkyres of Norse legend.

The ruins of a 17th-century house watch over the much older remains of Jarlshof

SHETLAND

The Shetland Islands are the most northerly part of the UK – early Roman writers, referring to *Ultima Thule*, 'the end of the world', almost certainly meant Shetland. The islands lie almost equidistant from Aberdeen, Torhavn in the Faroes and Bergen in Norway; Lerwick, the capital, is nearer to the Arctic Circle than to London. The archipelago of more than 100 islands, of which only around 20 are inhabited, is actually the tops of a range of hills that were drowned by the rise in sea level at the end of the last Ice Age. This is a distinctive and invigorating landscape of low-lying hills, peat-covered moors and water – a place where it is difficult, if not impossible, to ignore the forces of nature.

FETLAR

Fetlar is unusual amongst the Shetland Islands in being particularly fertile, as indicated by its Old Norse name meaning 'fat land'. It has a beautiful scenic coastline with a number of archaeological reminders of the past, from the Neolithic chambered cairn at Vord Hill to the Giant's Grave at Aith – a Norse burial site. The wildlife is remarkable and a large part of the island is an RSPB nature reserve. Fetlar gained recognition for the snowy owls which returned and bred there for a few years between 1967 and 1975. It is also important for its red-throated divers, beautiful, elegant birds which favour only the remotest places for nesting. Breeding auks and wintering wildfowl, together with seals and otters are just some of the highlights of the island's wildlife.

JARLSHOF AND ST NINIAN'S ISLE   Map ref HU4009

In much the same way as a great storm exposed the settlement of Skara Brae, so it was in 1905 that the ancient archaeological remains at Jarlshof at the southern end of Shetland were discovered. The site is dominated by the towering ruin of the 17th-century

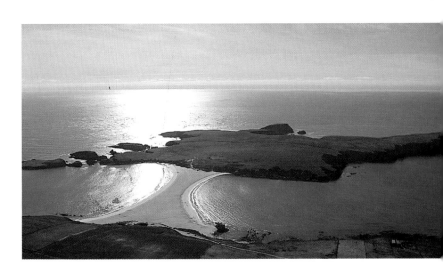

Laird's House, which overlies a prehistoric broch. This house was originally known as Sumburgh, until Sir Walter Scott renamed it 'Jarlshof' in his novel *The Pirate*. The name has stuck, and is now taken to refer to the whole site.

Jarlshof embraces Neolithic, Bronze-Age, Iron-Age, Pictish, Norse and medieval remains. A farm from the Viking period is particularly well preserved. The earliest Norse structure is the 9th-century Hall House, measuring nearly 69 feet (21 metres) in length, which had a central hearth, with low benches down each side and timber posts to help support the roof. Various extensions and modifications were made to this original design over the next four centuries. The succeeding medieval farm, built probably in the first part of the 14th century and inhabited until the end of the 15th, is a rare early example of a design of farm which was still being built in the 18th and 19th centuries. The dwelling house and byre were built parallel and close together, with a kiln for drying corn in the corner of the byre. As a record of human habitation in Shetland through the ages, Jarlshof is a supreme example.

Just up the west coast, lovely St Ninian's Isle is connected to the mainland by a tongue of white sand, or tombolo, which affords access for most of the time, except at exceptionally high tides. A small, beautiful, uninhabited island, this was where St Ninian, the first Christian missionary to travel to Shetland, made his base, although his main monastery was at Whithorn in Wigtownshire. The ruins of a medieval church, built in the 12th and 13th centuries on the site of a much earlier church, are still there. In 1958 a trove of Pictish silver was found under a stone slab beneath the nave, consisting of 28 objects, all beautifully worked and decorated (these are displayed in Edinburgh).

St Ninian's emerald island is linked to the mainland by a sand bar, or tombolo

THE PICTS

The Picts 'enter' into history in 279AD when the Roman poet Eumenius described the inhabitants of Northern Britain by that name, which means 'the painted ones'. These people can be considered as the true aboriginals of Scotland and are surrounded by many unanswered and unanswerable questions. What was their real name? What is the meaning of the series of symbols they have left as engravings? Whatever else, they were certainly talented craftsmen, able to work fine patterns into their silver jewellery and stone monuments. But what of the Pictish symbol stones? Are they memorials to the dead? Were they notices proclaiming territorial rights? Did they record allegiances formed by marriages? The final enigma, however, is what happened to the Picts? In the middle of the 9th century they disappeared from recorded history.

UP HELLY AA
The annual fire festival known as Up Helly Aa is held in Lerwick at the end of January. Although it is the creation of Victorian romanticism, it has important connections with the Viking heritage of the islands. The festival involves a torch-light procession through the streets of Lerwick, led by the ceremonial chief, known as the Geiser Jarl. The highlight of the festivities is the burning of a replica Viking longship, which is associated with the Viking tradition of placing their dead chieftain in a longship before setting fire to it to ensure his safe arrival in Valhalla.

Lerwick harbour is sheltered to the east by the island of Bressay

LERWICK   Map ref HU4741

Lerwick is the capital of Shetland and it is all because of fish. In the 17th century the sailing ships of the Dutch herring fleet found a safe haven in the waters of Bressay Sound, and trade with the crews brought prosperity to the Shetlanders. As more people came to capitalise on that trade, the settlement at Lerwick grew, stretching out along the coastline – the town's main thoroughfare, stone-flagged Commercial Street, still follows a tortuous winding route. This remains an area of great character and, as you wander, it is easy to imagine the hustle and bustle of those distant days. Look out for a local delicacy hanging in the butchers' windows – 'reestit mutton' is salt-cured, and gives a rich flavour to soups and stews. Another speciality is the knitwear – and nimble-fingered workers will even make you a garment to your own choice of pattern and colour.

The Dutch continued to have an effect on Lerwick – the oldest building in the town is Fort Charlotte, its construction in the 1660s prompted by the Second Dutch War. It is roughly pentagonal in shape, with a battery overlooking Bressay Sound, set behind a zig-zagged parapet. The fort saw no action, although in 1673 the garrison block was burnt by the Dutch, by now into their third war. It was only in 1780, when Britain was at loggerheads with Spain, France and the various states of Northern Europe, that the fort was completed and named Fort Charlotte after George III's queen. More recent building now encroaches on every side, and it is difficult to appreciate the scale of the structure from outside, but it is nevertheless well worth a visit.

If you want to seek out earlier inhabitants, you should make your way to the Iron-Age Clickhimin Broch, itself standing on the site of an even earlier Bronze-Age settlement, a mile (1.6 km) south west of Lerwick. It was occupied for about 1,000 years, and remains include a partially demolished broch which still stands to a height of 17 feet (5.2 metres).

The small island of Bressay protects Lerwick Harbour, acting as a natural barrier to the easterly winds and creating one of the safest anchorages in northern Europe. There is a regular ferry link between Bressay and Lerwick, enabling many of the people who live there to commute daily to work on the larger island. Bressay was an important fish processing centre during the boom years of herring fishing, but after its collapse in the 1930s the various factories closed. Today, the tradition of fish processing has been revived, with a modern fish-meal factory on the island at Heogan, but a large proportion of the fish that are caught in the waters around Shetland are taken by the fleet of rusty east European 'Klondykers' to be found anchored in Bressay Sound for much of the year.

Shetland has a rich tradition of fiddle music – catch a session at the famous Lounge in Lerwick, or listen out for a performance by the lively youngsters of Shetland's Young Heritage.

A supply ship in Lerwick harbour, which is also a base for North Sea oil rigs

NOSS NATIONAL NATURE RESERVE
The tiny island of Noss lies just to the east of Bressay and can be reached by a short boat trip across Noss Sound, where there is a good chance of seeing porpoises. There is a visitor centre and a waymarked walking route around the island, which is home to around 7,000 pairs of gannets, 6,000 pairs of fulmars, 7,000 pairs of kittiwakes and 40,000 pairs of guillemots, together with smaller numbers of razorbills, puffins, black guillemots and shags. The island consists mainly of moorland, covered with heather and crowberry, among which you will find heath spotted orchids, tormentil and thrift; spring squill grows along the cliff tops.

VIKING LAW

In Viking Shetland there were a number of districts, each with its own parliamentary assembly, or 'ting', which met to decide matters of ownership and settle minor disputes. These districts live on to this day in the names of some of the current parishes – Aithsting, Nesting, Delting and so on. Once a year representatives of these tings met at Law Ting Holm, once a tiny islet at the north end of Tingwall Loch, reached by a narrow causeway which can still be traced in the boggy ground. Here they would resolve any weightier matters and pass new laws. Similar systems were introduced in other areas, including the Western Isles and in the Isle of Man and Iceland, where the system survives to this day.

The harbour at Scalloway is dominated by the tower of the old castle

MOUSA AND SCALLOWAY

Mousa is a small, uninhabited island lying off the east coast of southern Shetland, and can be reached by a short boat trip from Sand Lodge Pier. It is a wonderful place to visit, not only for its superb wildlife – the island is designated a Site of Special Scientific Interest – but also for its broch dating from around 100BC to 300AD, which is widely acclaimed as the best preserved anywhere. At its base it is 50 feet (15.2 metres) in diameter, the walls are 43.5 feet (12.2 metres) high, and it has the typical twin-walled construction with an internal staircase. It is mentioned in *The Orkneyinga Saga* – Earl Harald arrived at 'Moseyjarborg' intent on battle with Erlund, who had abducted his mother, but the thought of trying to attack the broch quelled his ardour for a fight and the dispute was resolved by negotiation. Today the only squabbles are between neighbouring pairs of storm petrels, the smallest of Britain's seabirds, which nest in the holes in the walls.

Further up the long finger of southern Shetland, Scalloway was the medieval capital of the islands, and although today the seat of power has moved to Lerwick, it is still a town of notable importance. It lies at the centre of an historic area, with Tingwall, the centre of Norse administration, and the Loch of Strom, site of the ruins of the oldest castle in Shetland. Dominating the town is the spectacular ruined castle, built in 1600 by Earl Patrick Stewart but only inhabited for a few years before he and his son were executed in Edinburgh in 1615. Around 1640 it was occupied by a garrison of Cromwell's troops before falling into disrepair.

MUCKLE FLUGGA AND UNST

The name Muckle Flugga means 'big bird rock', and although many claim it is the most northerly scrap of the UK, just beyond it, to the north, lies Out Stack, to which this accolade truly belongs. The lighthouse on Muckle Flugga, which has helped steer boats around the northern tip of Shetland for over 100 years, was designed by Thomas Stevenson, the father of Robert Louis Stevenson, and completed in 1858. It is best viewed either at Saxa Vord or from Hermaness National Nature Reserve – and if you are lucky, you may also see, on a calm day, dolphins, porpoises or even killer whales breaking the surface of the water.

A ferry connects Unst with Yell and there is also an air service to the island. From Belmont, where the ferry docks, the road heads north passing the ruins of Muness Castle, the most northerly castle in Britain, and on towards Baltasound on the east side of the island. It was one of the principal herring fishing centres in Shetland between the 1880s and 1920s. Continuing north the road leads to Haroldswick with its pillar-box red Post Office, which is the most northerly in the British isles. There is an inescapable feeling of being on the edge of the world. Hermaness National Nature Reserve, in the north-west corner of Unst, is a brilliant gem in the treasure trove of Shetland wildlife sites. The cliffs, which rise to nearly 558 feet (170 metres), are home in summer to over 100,000 seabirds and the perpetual motion and continuous cacophony of sound with the backdrop of the North Atlantic offers a truly unique wildlife experience.

LIFE AT THE EDGE

The visitor centre at Hermaness National Nature Reserve is housed in the former lighthouse shore station, which was home to the families of the lighthouse-men of Muckle Flugga. It is run by Scottish Natural Heritage and offers an innovative introduction to the wildness of the landscape, the birds and the other wildlife of the reserve. A visit to the centre adds to the unique experience of the seabird cliffs themselves, giving a view from the base of the cliffs and the chance to see what it is like inside a puffin's burrow. Another summer attraction of the reserve is 'Albert Ross', the lonesome black-browed albatross who is sadly circling the northern hemisphere searching for a mate, all of whom are at similar latitudes in the southern hemisphere.

The lighthouse at Muckle Flugga, on its exposed rock

BLACK GOLD

Shetland history has always been inextricably linked to the sea – the Vikings arrived by sea to conquer and transform the land; fishing has always been important to the Shetland way of life – but nothing could match the discovery of North Sea oil for its impact on the islands. Sullom Voe is now the largest oil and gas terminal in Europe, its deep and sheltered waters providing a safe anchorage for the great supertankers which transport the crude oil all around the world. The oil gets to Sullom Voe by undersea pipeline, and the terminal handles on average a million barrels per day. Oil revenues have given Shetland new and improved roads, a new fleet of inter-island ferries and many new community centres and other public facilities.

An upturned boat provides an unusual roof on the island of Yell

WHALSAY AND YELL

Whalsay, just 5 miles (8 km) long and 2 miles (3.2 km) wide, lies 3 miles (4.8 km) east of the Shetland mainland, and its name is derived from the Old Norse, *Ivals-ey*, 'whale's island', probably because of its shape. Much on Whalsay is typical of Shetland as a whole – life is dominated by the sea, with fishing and crofting being the mainstays of the population of around 1,000. The great banks of peat are still cut by hand for fuel, and in the summer the bogs are striped by freshly hewn banks and the 'peats' stacked neatly to dry for the winter fires.

There is evidence of human occupation stretching back to the third millennium BC, best displayed at Pettigarth's Field, comprising two houses, Benies House and Standing Stones of Yoxie. The 17th-century Pier House at Symbister, a restored Hanseatic Böd, is a small two-storey building at the end of its own jetty, which served as both home and store. It has its own windlass, used to unload alcohol, tobacco, cloth and salt from German ships in return for dried and salted fish.

Yell is the second largest island in the Shetland archipelago. It gets its name from the Old Norse, *geldr*, meaning 'barren', and the description is still apt. At Gloup is an old fishing station, one of the biggest in Shetland in the 19th century, which stands as a stark and poignant reminder of the rigours of a past times. The sixerns, local boats so called because they were crewed by six men, used to hunt cod and ling in the deep waters 40 miles (64.4 km) offshore. Many men were lost to summer storms, and a memorial commemorates 58 men from 10 boats lost in 1881, who left 34 grieving widows and 85 fatherless children.

The Northern Isles

Leisure Information
Places of Interest
Shopping
Sports, Activities and the
Outdoors
Annual Events and Customs

Checklist

Leisure Information

TOURIST INFORMATION CENTRES

SHETLAND ISLANDS
Lerwick
The Market Cross. Tel: 01595 693434.

ORKNEY ISLANDS
Kirkwall
6 Broad Street. Tel: 01856 872856.
Stromness
Ferry Terminal Building, The Pier Head. Tel: 01856 850716.

OTHER INFORMATION

Ferries
Orkney Ferries, Shore Street, Kirkwall, Orkney. Tel: 01856 872044. Services throughout the islands.
P & O Scottish Ferries Jamiesons Quay, Aberdeen. Tel: 01224 572615. Daily sailings to Orkney from Scrabster (Thurso). Sailings from Orkney (Stromness) to Shetland (Lerwick). Also sailings from Aberdeen.
Shetlands Islands Council (Ferries). Tel: 01806 566259. Regular services throughout the islands.
Historic Scotland
Longmore House, Salisbury Place, Edinburgh. Tel: 0131 668 8800.

National Trust for Scotland
5 Charlotte Square, Edinburgh. Tel: 0131 226 5922.
Royal Society for the Protection of Birds
17 Regent Terrace, Edinburgh. Tel: 0131 556 5624.
Scottish Tourist Board
23 Ravelston Terrace, Edinburgh. Tel: 0131 332 2433.
Scottish Wildlife Trust
16 Cramond Glebe Road, Edinburgh. Tel: 0131 312 7765.
Weather
Great Outdoors Weatherline. Tel: 0891 567538. Mountaincall for north-west Scotland. Tel: 0891 505680. Western Highlands, climbing line – 5 day forecast. Tel: 0891 200819. Weathercall for north-west Scotland. Tel: 0891 500425.

ORDNANCE SURVEY MAPS

Landranger 1:50,000 sheet numbers 1, 2, 3, 4, 5, 6, 7, 18.

Places of Interest

There will be an admission charge at the following places of interest unless otherwise stated.
ORKNEY ISLANDS
BURRAY
Orkney Fossil Vintage Centre
Viewforth, Burray. Tel: 01856 731255. Open: Apr–Oct daily.

HOY
Dwarfie Stane
Tel: 0131 668 8800. Open: all reasonable times. Free.
Martello Tower
Hackness South Walls. Tel: 0131 668 8800.
Scapa Flow Visitor Centre
Lyness. Tel: 01856 791300 for details.

MAINLAND
Brough of Birsay
Eleven miles (17.7 km) north of Stromness. Tel: 0131 668 8800. Accessible only at low tide. Norse settlement, Romanesque church, replica of Pictish sculptured stone (original is in the Museum of Antiquities, Edinburgh). Open: all reasonable times. Free.
Click Mill
Dounby. Tel: 0131 668 8800. Open: all reasonable times. Free.
Earl Patrick's Palace
Kirkwall. Tel: 01856 875461. Open: Apr–Sep daily.
Earl's Palace
Birsay. 11 miles (17.7 km) north of Stromness. Tel: 0131 668 8800. Open: Apr–Sep daily.
Maes Howe Chambered Cairn
Off the A965, west of Kirkwall. Tel: 0131 668 8800. Open: all year daily, except Christmas and 1–3 Jan.

Orkney Farm and Folk Museum
North of Finstown. Tel: 01856 7712268. In two locations reflecting Island life before the turn of the 20th century. Open: Mar–Oct daily.

Orkney Natural and Maritime History Museum
52 Alfred Street, Stromness. Tel: 01856 850025. Open: all year daily except Christmas, New Year and 3 weeks in Feb/Mar.

Pier Arts Centre
Victoria Street, Stromness. Tel: 01856 850209. Open: all year most days. Free.

Rennibister Earth House
On A965, north west of Kirkwall. Tel: 0131 668 8800. Open: at all reasonable times. Free.

Skara Brae
Dounby. Six miles (9.7 km) north of Stromness. Tel: 0131 668 8800. Open: all year daily.

Stenness Standing Stones
Five miles (8 km) north east of Stromness. Tel: 0131 688 8800. Always open. Free.

Tankerness House
Broad Street, Kirkwall. Tel: 01856 873191. Open: all year most days. Free.

PAPA WESTRAY
Knap of Howar
On west side of Island. Tel: 0131 668 8800. A pair of 5,000-year-old buildings which have only just been recognised as one of the oldest sites in Europe, yielding whalebone artefacts and stone borers and grinders. Free.

ROUSAY
Midhowe Broch and Cairns
On the west coast, on a

Skara Brae was exposed during a fierce storm in 1850

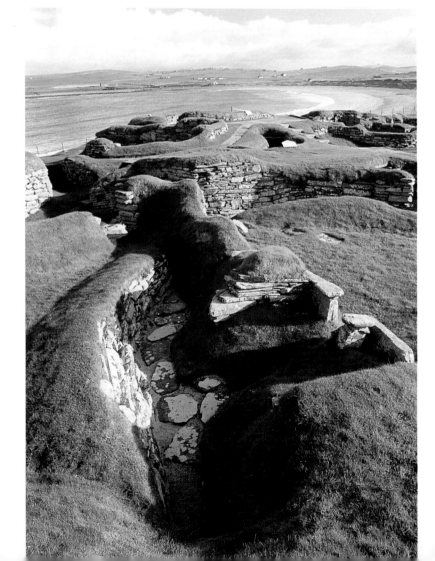

promontory cut off by a deep rock-cut ditch. Tel: 0131 668 8800. An Iron-Age broch and walled enclosure. Also Midhowe Stalled Cairn, 'an elongated ship of death'. Open: all reasonable times. Free.

SANDAY
Quoyness Chambered Tomb
On south coast, on the east side of Els Ness. Tel: 0131 668 8800. Open: at all times. Free.

SOUTH RONALDSAY
Tomb of the Eagles and Bronze-Age House
Liddle Farm, St Margaret's Hope. Tel: 01856 831339. Open: all year daily.

WESTRAY
Noltland Castle
Tel: 0131 668 8800. Open: at all reasonable times. Free.

FAIR ISLE
Fair Isle Bird Observatory
Charter flights or mailboat sailings (twice weekly) from Shetland. Tel: 013512 258251. Open: Mar–Oct.

SHETLAND ISLANDS
MAINLAND
Fort Charlotte
Lerwick. Tel: 0131 668 8800. Open: any reasonable time. Free.
Jarlshof Prehistoric Site
near Sumburgh Airport. Tel: 0131 244 3101. Open: Apr–Sep daily.
Scalloway Castle
Tel: 0131 668 8800. Always open. Free.
Scalloway Museum
Main Street, Scalloway. Extensive display of old photographs; the main display of local artefacts recalls the exploits of Norwegian resistance fighters who created the legendary 'Shetland Bus'.
Shetland Croft House Museum
Tel: 01595 5057. Open: all year most days .
Shetland Museum
Lower Hillhead, Lerwick. Tel: 01595 695057. Open: all year most days. Free.

Tingwall Agricultural Museum
Veensgarth off A971, 5 miles (8 km) north west of Lerwick. Tel: 01595 840344. Open: May–Sep daily, or by arrangement.
Up Helly Aa Exhibition
St Sunniva Street, Lerwick. Photographs of January Fire Festival and Viking longship.

MOUSA
Mousa Broch
Tel: 0131 668 8800 (01950 431361 to book boat trip from Sandwick). Always open. Free.

UNST
Muness Castle
South-east corner of Unst. Tel: 0131 668 8800. Open: all reasonable times (apply to key keeper). Free.

YELL
Old Haa Museum
Burravoe. Tel: 01957 82339. Open: Apr–Sep certain days. Free.

Shopping

LOCAL SPECIALITIES
ORKNEY ISLANDS
Distillery
Highland Park Distillery, Holm Road, on A961 near Kirkwall, Mainland. Open: all year weekdays; Jul and Aug daily. Tel: 01856 874619.

Sports, Activities and the Outdoors

ANGLING
There are ample opportunities for angling of all kinds. Enquire at Tourist Information Offices.

BOAT TRIPS
SHETLAND ISLANDS
Dim River
Lerwick Harbour, Mainland. Trips in a Viking longship. Contact Tourist Information Centre. Tel: 01595 693434.

CYCLE HIRE
ORKNEY ISLANDS
Orkney Cycle Hire, 54 Dundas Street, Stromness. Tel: 01856 850255.

GOLF COURSES
ORKNEY ISLANDS
Grainbank. St Ola by Kirkwall. Tel: 01856 872457.
Stromness Golf Club. Tel: 01856 850772.
SHETLAND ISLANDS
Lerwick Golf Club, Dale. Tel: 0159 584 369.

GUIDED TOURS
SHETLAND ISLANDS
Wildlife Tours. Scatness, Virkie. Tel: 01950 460254.

NATURE RESERVES
ORKNEY ISLANDS
Marwick Head Nature Reserve, Mainland. North from Marwick Bay. Tel: 01856 850 176/0131 5573136.
North Hoy Nature Reserve, North Hoy. Reached by boat from Stromness. Access at all times. Tel: 0131 557 3136.

SHETLAND ISLANDS
Hermaness National Nature Reserve, Unst. North end of island. Tel: 01957 711278.
Noss Nature Reserve, Isle of Noss. Tel: 01595 693345. Access by inflatable boat. Open: mid May–end Aug. Entrance charge.

WATERSPORTS
ORKNEY ISLANDS
North Isles Diving. Stromness (Subaqua). Tel: 01856 850832.
Skolla Diving Centre, Gulberwick. Tel: 01595 692175.

Annual Events and Customs

ORKNEY ISLANDS
Kirkwall
Ba' Games. Held on 25th December and 1st January.
Stromness
Orkney Traditional Folk Festival. Late May.
St Magnus Festival. Major British Music Festival, late June.
SHETLAND ISLANDS
Lerwick
Up Helly Aa, late January–early February.
Other local Up Helly Aa during February and March throughout Shetland.

Atlas and Map Symbols

The National Grid system covers Great Britain with an imaginary network of 100 kilometre grid squares. Each square is given a unique alphabetic reference as shown in the diagram. These squares are sub-divided into one hundred 10 kilometre squares, each numbered from 0 to 9 in an easterly (left to right) direction and northerly (upwards) direction from the bottom left corner. Each 10 km square is similarly sub-divided into one hundred 1 km squares.

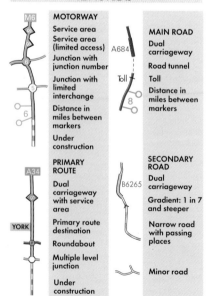

MOTORWAY		MAIN ROAD
M6		A684
Service area		Dual carriageway
Service area (limited access)		Road tunnel
Junction with junction number		Toll
Junction with limited interchange		Distance in miles between markers
Distance in miles between markers		
Under construction		
PRIMARY ROUTE		**SECONDARY ROAD**
A34		B6265
Dual carriageway with service area		Dual carriageway
Primary route destination		Gradient: 1 in 7 and steeper
YORK		Narrow road with passing places
Roundabout		
Multiple level junction		Minor road
Under construction		

✝	Abbey, Cathedral, Priory		Motor racing
🐟	Aquarium		Museum
⛺	Camp site	!	Nature or forest Trail
	Caravan site		Nature reserve
🏰	Castle	☆	Other tourist features
	Cave	✕	Picnic site
	Country park		Preserved railway
	Craft centre		Racecourse
	Garden		Skiing
▶	Golf course or links		Viewpoint
🏛	Historic house		Wildlife park
ℹ	Information centre		Zoo
✈	Aerodrome with customs facilities		Motoring organisation telephone
✈	Aerodrome without customs facilities		Public telephone
Ⓗ	Heliport		Radio or TV mast
	Lighthouse (in use and disused)		Windmill
	Light-vessel		

	Tour start point	Buckland Abbey	Highlighted point of interest
➡	Direction of tour		Featured tour
	Optional detour		

KEY TO WALKS

Scale 1:25,000, 2½ inches to 1 mile, 4cm to 1 km

	Start of walk		Line of walk
➡	Direction of walk	⠂⠂⠂⠂	Optional detour
		Buckland Abbey	Highlighted point of interest

ROADS AND PATHS

M1 or A6(M)	M1 or A6(M)	Motorway
A 31(T) or A35	A 31(T) or A35	Trunk or main road
B 3074	B 3074	Secondary road
A 35	A 35	Dual carriageway
		Road generally more than 4m wide
		Road generally less than 4m wide
		Other road, drive or track
		Path

Unfenced roads and tracks are shown by pecked lines

RAILWAYS

	Multiple track		Embankment
	Single track	Standard gauge	
			Tunnel
	Narrow gauge		Road over; road under
	Siding		Level crossing
	Cutting		Station

PUBLIC RIGHTS OF WAY

Public rights of way may not be evident on the ground

	Public paths { footpath / bridleway }	++	Byway open to all traffic
	Permissive path		Road used as a public path
		◆ ◆	Named path
	Permissive bridleway	Pennine Way	National trail or recreational path

The representation on this map of any other road, track or path is no evidence of the existence of a right of way

RELIEF

50 ·	Heights determined by	Ground survey
285		Air survey

Contours are at 5 and 10 metres vertical interval

SYMBOLS

■	Place of worship { with tower / with spire, minaret or dome / without such additions }	○W, Spr	Well, Spring
●			Gravel pit
+			
☐	Building		Other pit or quarry
☐	Important building		Sand pit
· T; A; R	Telephone: public; AA; RAC		Refuse or slag heap
--□-- pylon pole	Electricity transmission line		County Boundary (England & Wales)
△ △	Triangulation pillar		Water
⬗	Bus or coach station		Sand; sand & shingle
⌂ ⌂	Lighthouse; beacon		National Park boundary
⌖	Site of antiquity		Mud
NT	National Trust always open		
FC	Forestry Commission		

DANGER AREA
Firing and test ranges in the area
Danger!
Observe warning notices

VEGETATION

Limits of vegetation are defined by positioning of the symbols but may be delineated also by pecks or dots

♣ ♣	Coniferous trees	○ ○	Non-coniferous trees
○ ○	Orchard		Heath
⫟ ⫟	Coppice		Marsh, reeds, saltings.

TOURIST AND LEISURE INFORMATION

⛺	Camp site	PC	Public convenience
ℹ	Information centre	P	Parking
ℹ	Information centre (seasonal)	⚡	Viewpoint
🚐	Caravan site	⊕	Mountain rescue post
✕	Picnic site		

| 0 | 10 | 20 | 30 | 40 | 50 km |
| 0 | | 10 | | 20 | 30 miles |

Cape Wrath

Butt of Lewis

Port of Ness

A857

A858

A857

Stornoway

A896

Eddrachillis Bay

Scourie

A894

OUTER HEBRIDES

ISLE OF LEWIS

Scarp

Loch Langavat

A858

Enard Bay

A837

Lochinver

In

Le

A835

Taransay

Tarbert

Scalpay

Harris

Pabbay

Sound of Harris

THE MINCH

THE MINCH

Ullapool

North Uist

Lochmaddy

A865 A867

Sound of Monach

THE LITTLE MINCH

Fionn Loch

Gairloch

A832

Loch Maree

A835

Loch Fannich

Kinlochewe

A832

A896

Achnashee

A890

Rona

Uig

A855

A87

Loch Snizort

Sound of Raasay

Inner Sound

Benbecula

WESTERN ISLES

A850

Dunvegan

A87

Portree

A863

Raasay

Loch Monar

Loch Mullardoch

Can

South Uist

A865

ISLE OF SKYE

Drynoch

Kyle of Lochalsh

A87

R Alff

HEBRIDES or

Loch Langavat

Lochboisdale

Sound of Barra

A87

A87

A851

Sound of Sleat

R Garry

A87

Canna

Sound of Canna

Ardvasar

Loch Quoich

Loch Lochy

Barra

A888

Castlebay

Rum

Sound of Rum

Mallaig

Loch Morar

Loch Arkaig

A830

HEBRIDES

OF THE HEBRIDES

Eigg

Muck

Sound of Arisaig

A861

A861

Fort William

A82

INNER HEBRIDES

Acharacle

ORKNEY
ISLANDS

Rousay Eday
Stronsay Firth
MAINLAND
A967 A966 Shapinsay
A966 Kirkwall
Stromness A964 A960
South Ronaldsay

PENTLAND FIRTH

urness Strathy Point Dunnet Head John o' Groats Duncansby Head
Melvich Scrabster Thurso A836 A9
Bettyhill A836 Sinclair's Bay
Tongue Loch Loyal R Naver A897 A882 Wick
Altnaharra Loch Naver A895 River Thurso A9 Lybster
A838 Loch Shin

Unst
A968 YELL Fetlar
St Magnus Baa Yell Sound
Muckle Roe MAINLAND Whalsay
A971 Lerwick
Bressay
Foula West Burra

SHETLAND
ISLANDS

0   10   20 km
0   10 miles

Sumburgh Head

Lairg A839 Helmsdale
A837 A836 Golspie
Bonar Bridge A949 Dornoch
Tain Dornoch Firth

MORAY FIRTH

Alness A9 Lossiemouth Spey Bay Buckie Banff Kinnaird Head
Cromarty Cromarty Firth Elgin Portsoy A98 Fraserburgh
Dingwall A832 Nairn Forres A95 Keith A96 A981 A92 A952
A834 Fortrose A96 A941 Fair Isle Turriff A950
r of Ord A833 A862 Inverness A940 Charlestown of Aberlour A947 Peterhead
A862 A939 Dufftown A920 Huntly A948 A92 A952
Drumnadrochit Grantown-on-Spey A941 Ellon A975
A938 Oldmeldrum
Loch Ness Carrbridge A95 Inverurie A920
Invermoriston River Spey Alford A944 Kintore A947
rt Augustus Aviemore A939 A944 A96 Aberdeen
y Kingussie A9 A97 A980 A93
Newtonmore A86 A939 Aboyne River Dee Banchory A957
A889 Braemar Ballater Stonehaven
Loch Ericht

CAMPIAN MOUNTAINS

Blair Atholl Laurencekirk Inverbervie
A93 A837 A92 A90

HEBRIDES

SEA OF THE HEBRIDES

Canna

Sound of Canna

Rum

Sound of Rum

Eigg

Muck

Sound of Arisaig

Ardvasar

Sound of Sl

R Garry

A87

Fort Augustu

Invergarry

Loch Quoich

Loch Lochy

N

Mallaig

Loch Morar

A830

A861

A82

A86

Loch Arkaig

INNER HEBRIDES

Coll

Arinagour

Tobermory

Tiree

Scarinish

A848

Sound of Mull

Lochaline

A884

ISLAND OF MULL

A849

Loch Sengan

Fionnphort

Acharacle

A861

A861

A82

Fort William

Loch Linnhe

Ballachulish

A82

GRAM

A828

A85

Oban

Dalmally

Tyndrum

Killie

Firth of Lorn

Loch Awe

A819

Crianlarich

Lochearnhe

Loch Katrine

Loch A

Colonsay

Scalasaig

JURA

Sound of Jura

A846

Inveraray

A615

A83

A816

Lochgilphead

A886

A815

Loch Long

Loch Lomond

A8

A814

Port Askaig

A847

ISLAY

A846

Laggan Bay

Port Ellen

Tarbert

Kennacraig

Claonaig

Dunoon

A886

A844

Rothesay

Island of Bute

Largs

Dumbarton

A82

Greenock

A761

31

30

29

A78

Paisley

Gl

A760

K

A849

Gigha Island

A83

Lochranza

Brodick

ISLE OF ARRAN

Lamlash

A841

Campbeltown

Kilbrannan Sound

Ardrossan

Irvine

A71

A737

A736

A735

A77

Kilmar

Troon

Prestwick

Ayr

A719

A70

Maybole

Mull of Kintyre

A77

Girvan

A737

A760

Ballantrae

A714

N Gall

Loch Ryan

A718

Stranraer

A75

Newton Stewart

Gateh of Fl

Portpatrick

A77

A716

Wigtown

A747

A746

Whithor

Luce Bay

Drummore

Burrow

Mull of Galloway

| 0 | 10 | 20 | 30 | 40 | 50 km |
| 0 | 10 | 20 | 30 miles |

Index

Acknowledgements

The authors would like to thank the staff of the various Tourist Information Offices throughout the Highlands and Islands of Scotland, the Scottish Tourist Board, the National Trust for Scotland, and Caledonian MacBrayne Ferries for their invaluable assistance.

The Automobile Association wishes to thank the following photographers & libraries for their assistance in the preparation of this book.

D HARDLEY 13, 15, 17
THE MANSELL COLLECTION LTD 7e
NATURE PHOTOGRAPHERS LTD 6a (C Mylne)
SPECTRUM COLOUR LIBRARY 108, 115
CHARLES TAIT 104, 109, 111

All remaining pictures are held in the Association's own library (AA PHOTO LIBRARY) and were taken by J HENDERSON with the exception of the following pages 21 (A Baker), 3b, 9c, 10a, 11a, 11b, 68a, 72, 80, 85 (J Beazley), 20 (J Carnie), F/Cover, 3g, 32a, (S L Day), 3f, 7c, 7f, 9a, 10b, 10c, 81, 86, 102, 103, 105, 106, 107, 110, 112, 113, 114, 116, 118 (E Ellington), 6c, 7g, 8/9, 8c, 22, 32b, 62, 63, 64, 65, 68b, 79 (R G Elliott), 3e, 12a, (D Forss), 11c, 14, 16, 18, 56 (D Hardley), 6d (P Sharp), 89, 95, 96, 98 (M Taylor), 7d, 8a, 9b (R Weir), 3c (H Williams)